The Past is a Foreign Country

Alan Brown

To Berit

In gratitude for your loving companionship
over more than sixty years

Published in 2021 by Vantage Publishing Limited
9 Chestnut Suite, Guardian House, Godalming, Surrey GU7 2AE
www.vantagepublishing.co.uk

© Alan Brown 2021

ISBN: 978-1-8383469-3-5

INTRODUCTION

My Dear Grandchildren This Memoir is for you.

Several years ago I promised your parents - and your Grandma - that I would write a Memoir recalling important periods in my life, so that you would have a fuller account of your Grandpa than I had of mine.

From time to time I have been reminded of this undertaking, with more than a hint that, if I did not get on with it, I might run out of time - and you would be grievously disappointed in your Grandpa!

So here I am scribbling away, recalling some of my main experiences and reflections, in the hope that they may be of interest and value to you as you grow up to take an informed view of your family, your antecedents and the world of past generations (which will inevitably leave their influence on the world in which you will live and work).

It may be as well, at the outset, if I offer you some warnings, and some explanation, about the journey on which I have set out: its challenges and intentions.

First, I should emphasize that I have never (except when I was a conscript in the Navy during my national service) kept a diary to record my day-to-day observations about the events I have lived through. Indeed, I am suspicious of the motives of many diarists; and have never been able to persuade myself of the value to posterity of devoting much time to the keeping of a diary. Nor have I given much thought to maintaining some form of personal "archive" of documents which would help me recall the thoughts and actions of yesteryear.

The one important exception to these omissions is the voluminous correspondence with your Grandma as we became closer and closer (but were forced to live in different countries) during my time as a student at Cambridge and Cornell Universities between 1956 and our marriage in 1959. I am the last person to decry this source; and I am not ashamed to rely on quotations from it in this memoir. But you will understand that a cache of love letters over a quite limited period may not explore at all thoroughly what was going on in the wider world!

I have had to rely to a large extent on my memory in compiling the record outlined in these pages. And I don't need to remind you that memory is a fickle and unreliable instrument - even when the memoirist makes a brave effort to be open and frank (and honest with himself).

I am reminded of a passage in Julian Barnes's novel "Love Etc", in which one of the key characters observes that: "the story of our life is never an autobiography, always a novel... a sense of form, control, discrimination, selection, omission, arrangement, emphasis... that dirty three-letter word art".

Hilary Mantel, in her novel "Giving up the Ghost" offers a bleaker view of the task of the autobiographer. "Writing about the past", she says "is like blundering through the house with the lights fused, a hand flailing for points of reference... There are obstacles to bump and trip you, but what is most disconcerting is the sudden empty space, where you can't find a handhold and you know that you are stranded in the dark".

You have been warned. This is to be a very personal account of the events and emotions that seem to me, with hindsight, to have been most significant in influencing my behaviour and determining the shape of my career. But memory plays strange tricks; and there is much that memory does not record.

The title of this Memoir is drawn from LP Hartley's novel "The Go-Between", in which the elderly narrator reflects on his searing experience as a young schoolboy thrust uncomfortably into the role of messenger between a couple carrying on a clandestine affair. "The past", he noted, "is a foreign country: they do things differently there". In my case, the past treated in these pages involved no fewer than four countries. Before I settled down, in my mid-twenties to earn a living in the British civil service, I had spent more than half my years abroad: my first seven years in the Gold Coast (as it was called before it gained its independence as Ghana); at boarding school in Cape Town, South Africa for much of the Second World War; later on, following my undergraduate course at Cambridge, as a graduate student at Cornell University, USA; and finally, on my marriage to Berit, for a six month period in Sweden.

This early experience of "abroad" was not unusual among my contemporaries. Many grew up, as I did, in the UK's colonies, where their parents (and often their grandparents) had devoted much of their lives to administration and business in Britain's imperial possessions. For many, this led to separation from their parents to go to a boarding school in the UK for their secondary education. For many, as for me, their lives with their families were further disrupted by the Second World War. And after the completion of secondary education, most young men were conscripted into the armed forces , and spent much of two years' national service abroad - or at least far from the family circle.

Where my experience differed from most of my contemporaries was in choosing to study in America; and to marry abroad.

In this Memoir, I shall try to record, as honestly as my fading memory allows, the impact that these overseas ventures had on me; my impressions of the countries that gave me a temporary home; and some reminiscences about my education and about my ancestry.

The central fact about this experience, for me and many others like me, was the lengthy separation from home and family - as well as from England. This had an important impact on the family as well as on the (usually) sons who were "sent away". In my case the impact of separation was magnified by the fact that my father died shortly after retiring on health grounds from the colonial service and returning to England in 1947. I was then just short of my thirteenth birthday. I had not seen my father since May the previous year; and had all too little contact with him over the previous six years. I had learnt - had to learn - over these formative years to live my life largely without the close guidance and support of my parents. I shall have more to say about the effects this separation had on me in later chapters.

In setting off on this journey into the past, I initially intended to bring the journey to a close at the point I returned to Britain in 1959 after spending an idyllic summer in Sweden. After all, I thought, subsequent years have not included any extensive periods of living abroad; and my prospective readers - you - might have a very limited interest in details of my career in the British civil service!

On further reflection, I have concluded that it would be perverse to halt my journey before I had begun to earn my living, start a family or come face to face with some of the major problems the country had to confront in the political, social and economic fields in the 1960s and beyond. In part 2 of this memoir, therefore, I shall try to take my story forward to (about) the mid 1980s: that is, roughly, to the point where our children-your parents-- had themselves left home and started their adult lives and careers. It is for them to take the story of the family forward from that time.

THE WINTHROP PEDIGREE

In most families grandparents exercise a significant influence on the lives and attitudes of their grandchildren: sometimes by their pervasive presence; sometimes by the ways they interact with parents; and sometimes by their becoming stand-ins for parents for long or short terms. They can usually be relied on not only to influence standards of behaviour, but also to convey some understanding of the lives and loves of the families in which they themselves grew up.

I had little of grandparents' input.

My paternal grandparents scarcely figured. My father's father---also James Brown - was born and brought up in the Glasgow area, where he lived with his wife, Christine Ferguson, after their marriage, and where he was employed as a tailor. Christine died in the 1930s and grandfather succumbed in 1945: before I returned to Britain after the War. I can find no evidence that I ever met James, senior,or Christine; or that they made any moves to inhabit the lives of their English grandchildren during our short holidays in this country. It may be that my father did not strive to encourage that; and my father's early death closed down opportunities for me to discover something about his parents' lives and the relations with their 5 children (all but one of whom made their careers outside Scotland). Though I am by birth three-quarters Scottish, the influence of this blood on my life and loyalties has been very limited: I cannot claim Scotland as one of the "past countries" of this book!

My maternal grandparents were more of a presence. We must have seen something of them during periods home on leave from the Gold Coast in 1936 and 1938. After our return from South Africa at the end of the War, I lived briefly in their house in Brookwood in 1945 and again in 1946. But both grandparents were then in poor health. My grandfather died from cancer in 1947; and Granny suffered a succession of heart attacks in the following year. She passed away in 1949. These brief periods therefore provided very limited opportunities to establish close relationships with the grandparents or to learn much of their lives and careers. Moreover, my sister Shirley and I were probably too young to pursue questions I now wish I could answer.

My grandfather, Charles Frederick Winthrop (always known to the family as "Poppy") was born in 1875 to Captain Stephen Winthrop and his wife Louisa. He was not yet four years old when his father killed himself in a tragic accident with a shotgun; and his mother was left a widow with six sons (one not yet born) to care for. Though Louisa benefited from an allowance from her father-in-law, Reverend Benjamin Winthrop, she must have had great difficulty coping financially with the needs of her young children. She therefore moved from the family home in Painswick to Bedford to take advantage of the relatively modest school fees charged by Bedford School. In due course Poppy was enrolled at the school, and remained a pupil there until, at age sixteen, he entered HMS Worcester as an officer trainee for the merchant navy.

For the better part of the next ten years, Poppy's career was in the merchant navy, gaining experience as a second mate in both sailing and steamships. This career came to an end when he met, and became engaged to, Vanda Forbes, whose father was based in Southampton. At this point - perhaps through family contacts and influence - he was offered an appointment as superintendent of a tea estate in Ceylon (as Sri Lanka was called before it became independent). It was to the Hangranoya estate in the district of Nawalapitiya that he took his wife on their marriage in 1900; and it was there that his three daughters were born.(the youngest died when she was three years old).

Over the subsequent twenty plus years, Poppy managed two further tea estates, until he decided to return to England on retirement. This move was, I guess, prompted in part by the ending of the first World War (making sea journeys easier and more secure), but in larger part by his and Vanda's wish to rejoin their daughters (who had been sent home in their early teens to obtain their secondary schooling in England).

Though scarcely fifty years old on his return to this country, Poppy did not subsequently become employed again. He purchased a newly built house and became a "country gentleman": active on voluntary bodies until the Second World War called him to service in the Home Guard. By the time I came to know him a little better, he seemed older than his seventy years, though still the outgoing ,relaxed and affable character that he must have been in his younger days. He was not much given to dwelling on his past life - at least not with me. What he did leave me with was a strong sense of pride in his Winthrop family - and a family "Pedigree", which must have come down to him from his aunts. This document is in my hands to this day; and it provides an insight into aspects of the history of the Winthrop family from the time of Henry VII (I have to say that this document is not an easy read; though it is almost certainly based on a more authoritative Winthrop Family Pedigree compiled in 1874, there are some inaccuracies and misleading references that have drawn me to rely more on the 1874 version!)

From the various references to family history which I picked up from Poppy or from my aunt Barbara (Auntie Barbar, who was unquestionably the best source for family legends), I became most curious about the association with Governor Winthrop. He was the leader of what was called the Great Suffolk migration of Puritan "Saints"to America in 1630; and was elected Governor of the Massachusetts colony before he set sail for America (and subsequently was reelected twelve times).

He was undoubtedly one of the most influential figures in the early history of the United States.

A second question that is raised by the family Pedigree concerns the reason why our branch of the Winthrop family was usually referred to as the Irish Line: when did this happen and how long did the Irish connection survive?

Finally, I felt it important to discover the circumstances of great grandfather Stephen's death in 1879. Not surprisingly, perhaps, my grandfather showed no inclination to brief me on his father's demise.

In the following pages I shall provide what evidence I can on these questions; and I hope convey some insights about an aspect of English history. which has intrigued me for much of my adult life.

******

Early accounts of the Winthrops suggest that the family hailed originally from Northumbria; but moved in the late middle ages : first to Newark (there is a village of Winthorpe in Nottinghamshire which may have given its name to the family), and thence to London and to Suffolk. Certainly in the late 15th century there was an Adam Winthrop living in Lavenham, in Suffolk. His son, also Adam (born in 1498), was an ambitious clothier who acquired title to the Manor of Groton from the Crown in 1544 following the dissolution of the monasteries. This was a property of some 500 acres which had previously been part of the Lordship of the Abbot of Bury St Edmonds. The Winthrops thus became Lords of the manor of Groton; and like many gentry of that era became established as substantial landowners on the ruins of the monasteries.

Like many gentry, also, the family acquired a coat of arms, which was confirmed by the Garter King of Arms in 1592. This specifies: "Visor d'argent, 3 chevrons gules crenelles over a lion rampant sables, armed and langued. And for his crest or cognizance a hare proper running on a mount vert". The motto "Spes vincit thronum" was adopted in the early 18th century by John Winthrop FRS; and seems to have been embraced by the American line. There has been much speculation about the reason for this choice: including the ingenious suggestion that , in its English translation, it could be an anagram of John Winthrop. It's at least a plausible explanation!

Adam's offspring, by two wives, included William (born in 1524) and (yet another!) Adam(born 1553). It is from these two sons that much of my story proceeds: for William became in due course the founder of the Irish Line; and it was Adam's son, John (born 1587) who became governor of Massachusetts in 1629.

First, the Irish connection. On the next page I have attempted to compile a simplified presentation of those successors to William Winthrop who migrated to Bandon in County Cork and became prominent citizens in that county in the sixteenth and seventeenth centuries. William's oldest son , Adam (born in 1561) died in Ireland in 1634 ; and his younger brother Joshua also moved to Ireland in the early seventeenth century. So, too, did Adam's elder brother, John, who might have been expected to inherit the Suffolk estate but who agreed to give up his title when he decided to move to Ireland.

It seems likely that these three young men were among the early English settlers in what was termed the Plantation of Munster which took place from 1588. This was an era when England was taking greater control of Ireland and seizing opportunities for English investors to acquire property and position in Ireland by dispossessing the (mainly) Catholic families who previously owned the land. Adam and Joshua would have had little prospect of inheriting the Manor of Groton; and might therefore have been attracted to taking their chance in Ireland. Bandon , which was founded in 1604 and was a haven for Protestants, might have seemed an excellent base for ambitious young men looking to establish themselves as landowners.

The absence of parish records in Bandon makes it difficult to establish accurately the line of succession after John, Adam and Joshua. But it is certain that a Stephen Winthrop was living in Bandon in 1658; and the editor of the 1874 Winthrop Pedigree believed that he was

WINTHROP FAMILY PEDIGREE

ADAM WINTHROP(1498-1560)
Purchased Groton Manor 1544

Married (1)Alice Henry;   (2) Agnes Sharpe
    \\\   \\\
    \\\   \\\

                              John   **Adam(1548-**
    William (1529-1562)   **(1546-1613)** \\\
                                      \\\
                                   John

Married Eliz Norwood   m. Eliz Rysby 1587-1649
    \\\   Gov. Mass
    \\\   Died Ireland
Adam(1561-1634)   **Joshua**
m. Jane Hilles   m. Anne Norrington
Died Bandon
Offspring unknown   Offspring unknown
    \\\
    \\\
    \\\
Stephen of Bandon
Believed to be grandson
of Adam or John and living
in Bandon in 1658
    \\\
    \\\
Benjamin of Cork(1678-1725)
m. Bridget Pembroke
    \\\
    \\\
William (1705-1765)   **Stephen(1705-1763)**
    \\\   m. Frances Davie of Exeter
    \\\   \\\
                        \\\
Stephen of Pembroke   **Benjamin(1737-1809)**
                        m. Eliz. Neale
                        Gov. Bank of England 1804
                        \\\
                        \\\
                        Stephen(1767-1818)
                        \\\
                        \\\
                        Rev Benjamin(1800-1885)
                        m. Anne Thursby
                        \\\
                        \\\
                        Stephen(1839-1879)
                        Cap in 22nd Reg of Foot

probably a grandson of one of William's sons or of their half-brother John. Stephen's offspring included Benjamin of Cork (who was born in 1675, was sometime Mayor of Cork, and was buried there in 1729). Benjamin's son William was also Mayor of Cork(in 1747) ; and was credited with rescuing John Wesley from a mob which threatened to lynch him.

From this point in time, the close connection with Ireland appears to recede. Benjamin's children did not continue in Cork. His twin brother Stephen (born 1705), known as Stephen of Exeter, moved to London in 1720; and I can find no trace thereafter of members of the Winthrop family maintaining a residence in Ireland ,though Winthrop Street in Cork reminds us of the part the family may have played in 17th century Munster.

The family may be said to have become "repatriated" after little more than four generations; and thence came to form the main English line of Winthrops.

One of Stephen of Exeter's sons (inevitably Benjamin again!) became Governor of the Bank of England in 1804; and was resident in London throughout his career. His son Stephen was a medical practitioner in Tonbridge, where he was buried in 1819. Stephen's eldest son, Reverend Benjamin, was for many years Rector of Wolverton, near Stratford-on-Avon, and was a substantial and successful landowner in Warwickshire (who won prizes for his produce at agricultural shows).

It is fruitless to speculate why the Winthrops abandoned Ireland. They doubtless had many connections, business and family, in England; and they may have come to see a rosier future in the wealthier corners of this country. As successors of the Puritan tradition of 17th century East Anglia, they may have felt uneasy making their homes in Catholic Ireland, even though the conquest of Ireland by Cromwell's New Model Army paved the way for Protestant hegemony through much of Ireland. More likely, marriages into English families made a return to England seem the obvious way to cement relationships with prominent families.

******

There was a very different outcome of the Winthrops' venture to America!

In 1629 the chief investors in the Massachusetts Bay Company (who had obtained a Charter from the Crown to establish a new colony in America) approached John Winthrop (by then Lord of the Manor of Groton) with the proposition that he take on the leadership of the Company. After careful reflection he agreed to do so; and he was elected Governor of Massachusetts in October 1629. He gathered together a band of Puritan citizens and sympathisers with similar commitment to starting a new life in America; and they set sail in the Arabella in the following spring.

What led John Winthrop to this great leap of faith and hope? There seem to have been two main influences on his decision. First, he felt increasingly trapped by the economic slump across Europe (At the time of the Thirty Years War), which considerably reduced the income he could draw from his land. More importantly, he had become disillusioned at the aggressive stance of Charles I's government towards the Puritans and judged that he would be unlikely to obtain any Crown appointments to supplement his income. More generally, he felt that he would relish the opportunity to set up a new community in America , free of the constraints under which many Puritans suffered in early 17th century England.

On the voyage to America, Winthrop composed a lay sermon in which he set out his vision of the society of "Saints" he hoped to establish in New England. He pictured the colonists as in a Covenant with God to build "A City on a Hill with the eyes of all people on them". They must adopt a combination of group discipline and individual responsibility that would set a standard for all America. Despite the mighty changes that have taken place since Winthrop's day, these sentiments still resonate with the American people.

In my teens I became deeply interested in the impact this ancestor of mine had on American history. I even wrote an essay, which won the school history prize, on the ideas he developed about the relation of church and government in building a new society. Whilst I could never share his views about the essential bond between church and government, or achieve his spiritual conviction and commitment, I still see him as a model for leadership and faith in a new society. Though he struck many as excessively severe and sober in his relations with his people, his private correspondence with his wife, Margaret Tyndall , show him to have been an intensely loving and generous human being: no bigot and no autocrat.

John Winthrop was re-elected no fewer than twelve times as Governor of the Massachusetts colony and state .He died in 1648 having established a thriving colony with a number of tightly organized and well defended towns, each with its own church of "Saints". He never returned to England; indeed the Manor of Groton was sold when Winthrop sailed for America - and thus passed out of the Winthrop family's possession in 1630.

The influence of Governor Winthrop did not diminish on his death. His eldest son, alsoJohn, became the first Governor of Connecticut from 1654 to 1676, and thus extended the reach of the Winthrops across New England. Equally important, the Pilgrim Fathers' Mayflower community (originally settled at Plymouth as early as 1620) was absorbed into the Massachusetts colony in 1692, strengthening further the influence of Massachusetts on the development of the American colonies. Some historians came to see John Winthrop senior as one of the Founding Fathers of the United States.

******

The final element of this account of the Winthrops jumps over two centuries. But it has in common with the earlier sections of this chapter a past involving "another country."

Captain Stephen Winthrop, my great grandfather, was born in Snitterfield, Warwickshire in May 1839. He was the second son of the Rev Benjamin Winthrop; and, like many younger sons of that period, he looked to the army for a satisfying career. At the age of sixteen he purchased a commission as Ensign in the 22nd Foot, a regiment that had established a reputation as a successful fighting force in several overseas campaigns. Winthrop served in that regiment in several locations in Britain. But he seems to have become disillusioned with the lack of real military activity; and in 1862 resigned from the army by selling his commission.

By this time, the American Civil War (or "War of the States" as the Confederate side called it) was already under way; and Winthrop decided to throw in his lot with the Confederate army (whether out of sympathy for the Confederate cause or for the opportunity of active military service is uncertain). After some delay (I recall a letter to his parents recounting how the Northern navy intercepted his ship and sent Winthrop back to Britain), he arrived in Charleston, South Carolina in January 1863. He was assigned to a unit which was involved in the battle of Gettysburg.

The American Civil War Round Table published in 2016 an account of Winthrop's service in 1863 and 1864. This indicates that his debut as a Confederate officer was "inauspicious": he lost his way, failed in his assignment, and was put under arrest by his commanding officer! However, following his appointment to General Alexander's staff, he gained a reputation as a bold and brave officer, always on the look out for opportunities to challenge the enemy.

Most notably, in the Knoxville campaign in early 1864, he was commended for his gallantry in leading a charge "which had the happiest effect in leading the troops over the enemy cover". General Alexander describes the scene:

"I can see him now, in a short black velveteen shooting coat and corduroy trousers, with his rather short stout legs and high English seat in the saddle... urging his horse into a run... Winthrop dashed through a little gap in our line and right up at the breast work. he suddenly fell forward on his horse's neck, and the horse turned about in a curve and came back with him. He had gotten a bullet through the base of his neck tearing up the collarbone so that some inches of it had to be amputated".

Though Winthrop returned to active service after this injury healed, he subsequently left the Confederate army in 1865, before the War came to an end. He returned to England by way of Buenos Aires; and there met and became engaged to " a pretty English girl", Louisa Heath, whose family had settled in Argentina. They were married in 1867 and settled in Painswick Gloucestershire.

There was little prospect of Stephen returning to the British army; and there is no record of his taking up any other employment after his return from America. His retirement at the age of twenty eight must have been unsatisfying for an energetic and active individual with increasing family responsibilities. He must have relied to a considerable extent on the largesse of his father. This could well have preyed on his confidence about his future.

Might this provide some explanation for his tragic death in 1879, as a result of an accident with a shotgun? At the inquest, reported at some length in the Stroud Journal of 22 March 1879, the jury heard evidence about the unreliability of the gun Winthrop habitually used to shoot birds. They also had medical evidence from Winthrop's doctor about his depressed state of mind in the weeks before the accident. At the conclusion of the inquest the jury returned a verdict that "the deceased died from a gun shot wound, but there was not in their opinion sufficient evidence to show whether the occurrence was accidental or intentional".

Stephen Winthrop left behind a widow and five sons (plus a sixth not yet born). It is a sad fact that none of these sons produced a male heir to carry the Winthrop name into subsequent generations. This is in marked contrast to the numerous Winthrops who descended from Governor John Winthrop in the American line.

ACHIMOTA

Though I was born in England (at the Maternity Hospital in Woking, to be precise), I spent the greater part of my early years in the Gold Coast.

My parents were recruited to the staff of Achimota College in its early pioneering days. My father was appointed to be a master of arts and crafts , with a significant additional responsibility for the construction of the key new buildings for the College, in the late 1920s. This must have happened very shortly after he completed his training as a civil engineer at Glasgow Technical College: he cannot therefore have had much experience or preparation for the roles he was to play. My mother was offered the post of Mistress of Domestic Subjects in June 1931 (at a salary of £480 pa). She had had several years experience as a teacher of domestic science in Hampshire, which must have counted in her favour with the authorities in the Colonial Office. She travelled out to the Gold Coast in the late summer; and I believe she met her husband-to-be on the sea voyage to Accra. They would be married in the College Chapel in May 1933.

By that time, the College had been going for less than five years. Its foundation and ethos owed much to three remarkable men, who defined its mission for the advancement of educational opportunities in the Gold Coast.

Sir Gordon Guggisberg was appointed Governor of the Gold Coast in 1919 after a distinguished war service. He had wide experience as soldier and administrator in West Africa; and had a profound knowledge of, and affection for, the people of the Gold Coast. He quickly identified the need for a significantly greater Government investment in education,(which in 1919 amounted to only £55000); and he set up a Committee to advise on education priorities. That Committee recommended the establishment of a secondary boarding school for boys on a site of about 3 square miles in the village of Achimota, about 6 miles north of the capital Accra. In the following seven years Sir Gordon extended the terms of reference of the proposed College and persuaded both the British government and other interested parties of the need for the college. At his retirement after the College opened its doors in 1927, it was said of Guggisberg: "If ever a man erected his own monument, that man is Guggisberg. His name will be joyfully handed down from generation to generation".

Just as important as Guggisberg's influence on Government support and commitment was the appointment in 1924 of the first Principal and Deputy principal: Rev AG Fraser and Dr James Aggrey. Fraser came to Achimota after twenty years as Principal of Trinity College at Kandy in Ceylon; and with a wealth of experience in adapting the ethos of a British public school to the needs and culture of another people. He was convinced that there was no reason to believe that the abilities of the African were inferior to those of any people in the world. As Africa had made a late start in developing education opportunities "only the very best was good enough". He believed, moreover, that it was essential to have a strong body of Africans on his staff, with the qualifications and character to contribute to the College's objectives. His emphasis on "character training", thoroughness in work and practical service in the community were aspects of his leadership that set the tone of the College's work. He was always known as "the Chief " - indicative of the respect he earned with both staff and students.

James Aggrey, the Deputy Principal, was born in the Gold Coast. He had already built up a reputation as a man of formidable ability at a Methodist School in Cape Coast, when he was selected to be trained in the United States as a missionary. He studied at Livingstone College in North Carolina, and graduated from there with three degrees in a range of subjects. Later on he earned a doctorate in divinity; and continued his academic career in America until, in 1920, he was persuaded to make a tour of Africa to study what might be done to improve education throughout the continent. It was here he came to the notice of Guggisberg, who recognised the contribution Aggrey could make to Achimota. Hence his appointment as Deputy to Fraser in 1924.

Possibly the most significant contribution Aggrey made was in his insistence from the outset that Achimota should be co-educational. He famously argued: "The surest way to keep people down is to educate men and neglect the women. If you educate a man you simply educate an individual; but if you educate a woman you educate a family and a whole nation". Guggisberg and AG Fraser were persuaded of the case for girls to be enrolled at Achimota; and this became a core part of the College's mission.

Aggrey's influence was also important in emphasising the need for collaboration of black and white in the development of Achimota. He said: "You can play a tune of sorts on the white keys, and you can play a tune of sorts on the black keys; but for harmony you must use both black and white." From this simple truth, Aggrey proposed the logo of the College as a piano keyboard, which was quickly accepted as the emblem of Achimota (and so it has remained!). It was a tragedy for the College that Aggrey contracted meningitis in 1927 while on a study course in America, and died before he could return to his post in Achimota.

These three men thus came to share a vision for the College, which embraced the following central principles:
- the College should provide for teaching from kindergarten to university levels;
- there should be a strong emphasis on teacher training;
- staff should be recruited from the European and African communities;
- the College should provide boarding accommodation so as to be able to enrol pupils from the whole of the Gold Coast;
- the College should be co-educational.

To these principles was added the decision, endorsed by the Colonial Secretary in London, that the College should be independent of the government and run by a Council. The Council was to have representation from staff and students, African and European, as well as appointees of the Government. A constitution affirming this arrangement was formally underwritten by the Achimota Ordinance, which came into effect in April 1930, amid great celebration (it was described as "one of the greatest educational steps Africa has yet taken").

I was, of course, much too young to appreciate the merits and strengths of this foundation, for Achimota and for the Gold Coast. But by the time that I arrived on the scene, I would have been able to observe at least some of the main buildings that had been completed and come into use. Of these the most prominent to a very young child were the bungalows built to house the senior staff and teachers, and the swimming pool (the construction of which had been managed by my father, and had cost less than £1000!).

The residential buildings were set on concrete pillars well above the ground, with their kitchens in a separate block at ground level (and an outdoor breakfast area under a thatched roof). The children's bedrooms had wire-netting windows which kept out mosquitoes but allowed a flow of air to freshen the rooms. When we were not indoors, we children spent much of our time in the swimming pool, or on the tennis courts, or on the large field (where my father taught me to ride a bicycle). At weekends, we would often be driven to the beach hut on the coast east of Accra. My sister Shirley (18 months my junior)and I met up frequently with other children of the teachers and senior admin staff; and we felt very happy and comfortable with the social life these contacts offered. The occasional children's party took us into Accra; but this was not a frequent event. The Achimota compound usually met all we wished for - though the family were able to spend several holidays in the guest house in Aburi ,where the luxuriant plant life offered an attractive change from the generally parched character of Achimota.

Although the kindergarten classrooms in the Western compound must have been operational by the time I reached school age (in 1939), I have to admit that I have no recollection of going to school. It seems to me now that much of my education took place at home: reading Beatrix Potter's books, or Babar The Elephant by Jean de Brunhoff, or AA Milne's series of Winnie the Pooh stories, or Shockheaded Peter's warnings about the consequences of naughty or obstinate behaviour. By the time that I left the Gold Coast, I was certainly an avid and fluent reader with a developed taste in particular for the whimsical poems of Milne. On the other hand, my writing was confined to block capitals: a severe handicap when I moved to school in Cape Town.

At about the time I reached school age, two developments disturbed the routine of our lives.

First, at 7.20 pm on 22 June 1939, the Achimota compound was shaken by a severe earthquake which hit much of the coastal area of the Gold Coast. I vividly remember the shock of our bedroom seeming to bounce furiously up and down as though the whole house was about to collapse. My parents rushed in to rescue Shirley and me from the threat of such a collapse; and for the next ten days we camped under canvas in the garden, in case the forty or more aftershocks should cause more damage . In fact, almost all the concrete buildings at Achimota survived with remarkably little damage. But the earthquake had a profound effect in Accra, where a large number of mud-built homes were destroyed or made uninhabitable. Much rebuilding was necessary: using tiles made in the workshops of Achimota. My father was lent by the College to the Gold Coast government to help in the rebuilding work.

The second development had a more serious and long-lasting effect. The Second World War broke out in September 1939; but for the better part of two years it did not impinge too seriously on life at Achimota. But from about the last part of 1940 it began to strike home. Many of the British and African teaching staff joined up with the army. Those who remained at their post were forced to take their appointed leave in South Africa because the uboat campaign made it impossible to risk taking their leave in the UK. Others decided to take retirement or move to alternative, and presumably safer, locations. By mid 1941, it was reported that only four white children remained on the compound. During the next two years, moreover, much of the Achimota accommodation on the Western compound, was taken over by the army and by the staff of the Resident Minister (Lord Swinton) who was sent to the Gold Coast to ensure that the country was on a proper war footing, providing intelligence etc to the War Cabinet.

I was a "victim" of this development. My parents were due to go on leave in mid-1941; and they elected to take the family to Cape Town for their holiday. Since they had concerns about the effects of the dislocation resulting from the war, they decided that I would be both safer and better educated if I was enrolled in a boarding school in South Africa. When they and Shirley returned to Achimota in August 1941, therefore I was left behind to enter St Georges Cathedral School in Cape Town.

I am left with one memory of that exodus to South Africa. On the sea voyage, my solar topee - standard headgear for all colonials living in the tropics - was blown off my head as I was playing on the deck of the ship. It struck me at the time as the end of my early years, and as an omen that it was time to start a new journey.

SOUTH AFRICA

The family arrived in Cape Town in June 1941, after an uneventful voyage. We checked in at a guesthouse, St Georges, in Claremont, a mainly residential area on the outskirts of Cape Town. Our landlady was Mrs Ludwig - always known to us as Granny Ludwig - a lady in (I guess) her early sixties, and a widow with four grown up sons. We were to share the single storey accommodation with the eldest son, Olver, and his wife and family.

Granny Ludwig appeared at first rather a dour disciplinarian; but we soon discovered that she was a kindly and considerate hostess with a heart of gold. From the first she made us feel welcome; and looked after us during the six weeks or so we stayed at St Georges as members of her family. We established good relations with her sons (and their wives) who soon took us on visits to outlying townships and winegrowing areas. My sister Shirley and I also quickly made friends with Olver and Peggy's two elder daughters, Marlene and Cynthia. The Ludwig family thus gave us the most agreeable introduction to South Africa; and many of the links with them continued long after our initial stay in the country came to an end.

Though we landed in Cape Town in the middle of the winter, when the weather is typically wet and windy, my recollection is of a succession of mostly fine days and cool nights, which offered a welcome contrast to the hot and humid conditions that we left behind in the Gold Coast. We particularly enjoyed visits to the beautiful botanical gardens at Kirstenbosch; though, surprisingly, we did not find the opportunity to take the cable car up Table Mountain, which provides the most spectacular viewing point over Cape Town (it was to be several years before I remedied this omission!).

Daddy's leave extended only to the beginning of August; and it was clearly my parents' intention to return with Shirley to the Gold Coast when the holiday came to an end. Shirley was much too young to be left at boarding school in the Cape. I don't know whether plans had already been made for my future education before leaving Achimota; but it soon became clear that my parents must have made arrangements with the Headmaster of St Georges Cathedral Grammar School for me to attend that school as a boarder when they returned to Achimota.

I was not privy to these consultations; and at no time was I given the opportunity to visit the school. But I was excited by the smart uniform I was to wear; and felt proud and grown up when photographed outside our lodgings as we set out on the short journey to Mowbray, where the boarding establishment of St Georges School was located. I had little idea what I was in for!

On the appointed day, I was ushered into the Headmaster's room and introduced to Rev Cecil Tugman and his wife Mary. They were friendly and welcoming; but it was not long before my parents said their goodbyes, and I was led across the hallway to the dining room for the evening meal. There I was confronted with, I guess, some sixty fellow boarders, aged between 8 and 18. None of this multitude had been deputed to show me around and introduce me to the school routines. It seemed to me that I was on my own!

The scanty introduction gave me little opportunity to take the measure of my new "home from home" or of the regime which I would be governed by. Over the next few weeks and months I slowly and nervously took note of some of the basic facts about St George's Grammar School.

The School had been founded in 1848, at the initiative of the newly appointed Bishop Robert Gray, on a temporary site close to the Cathedral (with which it was to be closely linked). Initially, it was intended to be a school for pupils of 8 to 12 years of age; but after about 10 years it was decided to introduce classes leading to the Matriculation exam at age 18. For most of the early years numbers of pupils enrolled varied from about 170 to as few as 40 - reflecting the perceived quality of the head and teaching staff and the difficulties of catering on the restricted site alongside the Cathedral for expansion (especially to provide for more boarders).

There were several proposals to expand the school's accommodation in the late nineteenth century. But it was not until Cecil Tugman was appointed headmaster in the 1930s that a determined effort was made to acquire premises for boarders. Tugman took the initiative to acquire the Bloemendal site in Mowbray, together with a former Priory, to enable the school to take around 50 boarders. The estate included a 300 year old gabled Dutch-style manor house and 43 hectares of land stretching down to the Liesbeck river. A new wing was added to the manor house; and in 1938 the first group of 40 boarders moved in. Tugman enthused:"She is our promised land and we thank God for our home, after years of wandering in the gardens".

It was this Dutch-style building which confronted me on my arrival in Mowbray in August 1941; and which was to be my base for the following three years plus. The main house provided the necessary accommodation in two largeish dormitories; whilst a rather ramshackle timber structure served as a space for doing homework. There was also a chapel; and rough and ready playing fields for rugby and cricket (which were flooded by the river on more than one occasion).

One consequence of establishing the boarding accommodation in Mowbray, some 10 miles outside Cape Town, was that the boarders had to commute daily by train into the centre of Cape Town to attend lessons in the main school buildings. The younger boarders would therefore march in "crocodile" each morning the half-mile to Mowbray Station.

The early months following my arrival at St George's School were the most uncomfortable and daunting of my life. My parents had departed and left me - so it seemed - to the mercies of my fellow pupils. I felt alone. I knew little of the customs of the school or the boarding house. I was the youngest pupil: about a year younger than anyone else. I had joined my class (Standard 1) midway through the academic year, when all the others in the class had established friendships and cliques which were effectively closed to me. There was no obvious friend or grown up I felt I could turn to. Every aspect of the daily round seemed charged with horrors; and for over a week I did not dare to enter the lavatories to empty my swollen bowels. I was also, predictably, wide open to bullying: to taunts and slights ; to being pushed around and scored off; and to some physical assaults. I lived in constant fear of being punished by one of the prefects, whom I saw consistently armed with canes. I was too timid and ashamed to seek help from the masters with responsibility for discipline in the boarding house.

In sheer desperation, I took what proved to be a "life-enhancing" step. I wrote a long and tearful letter to Tom and Joan Watkins, close and supportive friends from Achimota, who were staying in the Cape on an extended holiday. I explained my anxieties and asked their help. They knew me well enough to credit what I wrote. They must have taken swift action to inform the headmaster of the state I was in. The Tugmans, too, responded sympathetically to my plight - and probably read the Riot Act to the boys largely responsible for the bullying. More importantly, they gave me much moral and practical support, which made me feel that I had friends I could turn to. I am forever grateful to the Tugmans - and of course my Auntie Joan and Uncle Tom Watkins - for their actions in rescuing me from something near to despair. I was also grateful to Mary Tugman for the concern and kindness she showed me when I suffered several infections and illnesses around this time. I well remember her watching over me as I had a chloroform glove placed over my frightened face in the course of treatment for a severe ear infection! At one point , in January 1942, I had a bout of bronchitis, and the doctor advised that I should not risk spending the next winter in the Cape.

I slowly - very slowly - got back on to an even keel. Though I remained somewhat timid and cautious, and slow to form close friendships, I came to believe that I was making sufficient headway in the classroom to gain some credit with my teachers and fellow pupils. I was sufficiently resilient, and sufficiently optimistic, to think things could improve.

My "rehabilitation" was reinforced by two further factors.

When I returned to school at the beginning of the new academic year in January 1942 - after a morale-boosting Christmas holiday with the Watkins family at Melton Wold-- I rejoined the admission class (Standard 1) , but with an entirely new set of classmates. My former "tormentors" had all moved up to the next class. The newcomers were of much the same age and academic standing as myself. It was much easier for me to begin to form lasting friendships with them. This change was in many ways the turning point in my school life.

Equally important was the encouragement I was to get from two outstanding teachers. Mrs Pearce was the class teacher for Standards 1 and 2. She has been described (by the historian of the School, Patrick Coyne, in his book "Cross of Gold") as "a tiny, ancient, wrinkled old lady, with arms as thin as matchsticks, who looked as though she couldn't hurt a fly". In truth she was much younger and more vigorous than her old-fashioned pince-nez spectacles and slender frame suggested. She was a gifted teacher, who understood how to get the best out of well motivated young people; and she had no difficulty keeping discipline among the less motivated. She excited in me a strong interest in the English language, and especially in poetry, which has remained throughout my life.

I can recall one incident that illustrated the advance I made under Mrs Pearce's benign influence. She was wont on occasion to set up a so-called "Spelling B" to test the class in spelling more difficult words. We would form a queue, and the pupil at the head of the queue would be asked to spell a word; if he succeeded, he remained at the head; if not the next in line would have the opportunity to spell the word correctly and go to the head of the queue. On this occasion, I was in the middle of the Spelling B queue, when the word MYRTLE was called out. I was the only pupil who was able to spell it correctly; so I moved to the head of the queue. I was not displaced from that position for the rest of that year. My position at the top of the class in English became secure; and subsequently I was awarded the form prize. I felt I had arrived!

However, my handwriting was a handicap: when I started at St George's, I could write only in block capitals! Mrs Sohr was deputed to take me in hand. A contemporary of mine, who was also taught by Mrs Sohr, described her "as a terror... whose temper varied as the weather". Her pet subject was handwriting. I had to learn to hold my pen in exactly the right way, and to produce exactly the right angle of copperplate which she demanded. I would repeat a dozen times a simple word or phrase precisely within the horizontal lines on the page she provided; and I did not move on to a fresh word until Mrs Sohr was entirely satisfied with my efforts. Though she was unquestionably a demanding teacher, and for many an intimidating presence, her methods were effective - and in my case resulted in my being awarded the school's writing prize at the end of my second year.

By that time I had been promoted to Standard 3 (Mrs Pearce having applauded my success under her supervision in Standards 1 and 2 and recommended my promotion). Miss Holder was the class teacher for Standard 3. She was younger and more approachable than either Mrs Pearce or Mrs Sohr, and her style was more informal and relaxed. She was the ideal character to give me the encouragement to build on the success I had achieved. I recall doing reasonably well in Afrikaans, which was a compulsory subject for all pupils in the School. I even scored well in mental arithmetic! At the end of the school year, in December 1943, I again carried off the form prize (a book by Enid Blyton), and gained promotion to Standard 4.

Academic progress was of course only one side of the school's objectives. Like other private boys' schools in South Africa, a good deal of importance was attached to success on the playing fields, in rugby and cricket. Whilst I became an enthusiastic cricketer, with some success with the bat, my recollection is that for the younger boys the development of skills was not given much priority - nor was it well organised. Surprisingly, I can remember no occasion I took part in a competitive game of rugby or even an organised coaching session. Whilst the more senior boys competed in matches with other schools, the lack of playing fields of good quality seems to have left limited opportunities to develop prowess among the juniors. My one prize on the playing field was to win the wheelbarrow race in the school sports held at the Newlands cricket ground (was it in December 1943 or 1944?).

Living within a boarding school, with very limited contacts with the world outside, and at a relatively young age, my experiences of the wider society of South Africa were very limited. I was well aware of the strict divide between whites (often called "Europeans") and "non-whites" (which included both people of mixed race who were usually described as "coloured" and were prominent in areas around Cape Town, and "blacks") in almost all public places. I well recall the shocked reaction I provoked on the occasions I played football with the coloured "boy" who was employed on gardening and housekeeping tasks at Granny Ludwig's house. The full rigour of Apartheid was not introduced until after the general election of 1948 handed political power to the Nationalist Party. But the basic attitudes of the white community towards association with Blacks were already firmly entrenched.

St George's School was wholly white - though in its early days there was a handful of non white pupils enrolled. There was never any mention of opening doors to bright black or coloured boys during my time in Cape Town. In the 1960s the School's Governing Council refused to enrol the ten year old son of a coloured clergyman who sought to test the Christian commitment of St Georges; and it was not until 1978 that the first non-white boy was enrolled at the School.

Thereafter the move to a multi-racial approach took off. In 1981 the Sunday Tribune journal published an article under the banner headline: "School for the colour-blind", and commented on the School as "an island of extraordinary racial harmony" At that point 30% of the 270 boys in the School were non-white. The collapse of Apartheid - and no doubt the prayers of a black Archbishop Desmond Tutu - reinforced the School's moves towards becoming the unashamedly multi-racial (and, incidentally, coeducational) institution it now is.

This reference to the influence of Desmond Tutu brings me back to the association of the School with the Anglican Cathedral and the Anglican principles it promoted. How far and how deeply did the physical presence of the Cathedral instil in the ethos of the School (and in me) the fundamentals of the Church of England?

In its early years, the headmasters appointed usually had a responsibility, as Precentors, for sustaining the musical standards of the Cathedral; and they were often ordained clergymen. Many of the school's pupils served and sang in the Cathedral choir. The whole school gathered in the Cathedral for morning prayers and hymns before the start of lessons - and the chosen hymnal was the English Hymnal (edited by Ralph Vaughan Williams). The services and sermons that took place at Bloemendal reinforced the Anglican traditions. Though there were among the pupils a number of expatriate Greeks, who would presumably have been more familiar with the rites of the Greek Orthodox church, the School made no concessions to "nonconformists".

For me, the school introduced me for the first time to the language of the St James's Bible and the Book of Common Prayer: in other words to the language and rhythms of Shakespeare and Tyndale. They had a profound impact on my juvenile sensibility. Long after I began to doubt some aspects of the Church's teaching , the sheer beauty of the phrasing of these seminal 17th century texts continued to rouse strong emotions. They still bring back memories of standing in the hall at Bloemendal at evening prayers to hear the headmaster or chaplain reading the familiar and well loved prayers: "Lighten our darkness we beseech thee, O Lord" and the rest. My agnosticism cannot dislodge the resonance of these words!

For much of the period I was a pupil at St George's my parents remained in Achimota. I relied for my holidays on a succession of parents of fellow pupils, and on Joan and Tom Watkins (who, by some good fortune, seemed always to be ready and available to welcome me to their family circle: at Melton Wold in April 1942; in Halesowen in 1943; and at Queenstown in 1944. Halesowen I remember with greatest clarity, partly because Tom wrote an account of it for his daughter Jenny. This made much play of the fun we had with a dog called Maleish: a retriever, I think, and certainly a dog with a great fondness for diving into the water for our delight to try to retrieve stones we cast in for him.

I think now that Joan and Tom regarded me as a kind of foster son, who would be good company for their daughter Jenny (who was about the same age as me, and had no brother or sister). Whatever their motives, they showed me always a great deal of consideration and affection, which made the absence of my parents bearable.

At the beginning of 1943 my father was due a further period of leave. He and my mother and Shirley therefore returned to Cape Town, and rented a house , again in Claremont, for what would be the school's autumn holiday. "Tsalta" was a generous-sized house which provided an ideal place to spend my holiday --and celebrate the fact that the family were united again under one roof and would be around for the celebration of my ninth birthday.

In the course of that holiday, my mother confided to me, as I crept into her bed one morning, that she had decided to accept the post of

Matron at Bloemendal. The reason for this decision was evidently to enable her to keep a close eye on me – and on Shirley, who was to be enrolled at a girls' school in the area. Thus it was that at the end of the holiday, my father returned to the Gold Coast on his own, and my mother took up post as Matron, with her bedroom and " consulting room" just below my dormitory.

I was of course delighted - if occasionally embarrassed! - to have Mummy close to hand - and to have her read stories to my dormitory mates before we went to bed .

The task of Matron was probably not too onerous; but it must have been difficult for her to be apart from her husband for an indefinite period and missing out on the interesting duties she had expected to take on as a member of the Resident Minister's staff in the Gold Coast. Shortly after Christmas 1943 she therefore resigned her post as Matron and returned to Achimota. By then I felt myself to be a well established and reasonably confident member of the school and boarding house community. Shirley, too, was fairly happily settled at boarding school. This parting may therefore have been more painful for Mummy than for Shirley and me.

Some while before Mummy returned to Achimota, she took an important decision about my academic curriculum. She arranged that I should have lessons in French rather than continuing with Afrikaans. I assume that she was advised on this course by Rev George Oakley, housemaster at Bloemendal. Himself an expatriate, he would have been aware that when I returned to England I would find French a standard part of the school curriculum; and that I would be at some disadvantage if I did not set about learning French as soon as possible.

At all events, in 1943 I started classes in French with Mrs Wallenkamp. She was Dutch, not English or Afrikaner or Huguenot. This had a significant advantage: her pronunciation of French words would not have the typical faults that many English pupils were prone to.

There were to be only two pupils in the classes with Mrs W: the other one was John Honey, also an expatriate who was expected to return to England at the end of the War. I don't know whether Mrs W had any responsibilities for teaching older boys; but as far as John and I were concerned we had her to ourselves; an extraordinary advantage.

I never knew who paid for these lessons. With hindsight, I must assume that my parents - and John's - must have footed the bill, not the School. Whoever paid, it was money well spent.

My parents were back in South Africa shortly after Christmas 1944. I had spent the Christmas break with the family of the Vicar of Stellenbosch, father of Arthur Brown, a school friend of mine. My parents drove down to Stellenbosch to take me back to Claremont to stay once again with Granny Ludwig. It was at this point that I became a day boy - and remained so until the war in Europe came to an end, and it became possible for expat families to plan their return to England. My time at St Georges School came to a close in July 1945, and Mummy , Shirley and I booked a passage to Liverpool on SS Tyndareus in (I think) early August. Before that, my father had returned once again to the Gold Coast; and we would not have him with us until the start of our Easter holidays in 1946.

How to sum up m.y experience of approximately four years as a schoolboy at St Georges and an expatriate child in South Africa?

I had, of course, grown up significantly: become more confident of my ability, better able to relate to my peers and school masters, and to achieve progress in the classroom and on the cricket pitch. I had learned to fend for myself - though with much support from family friends, and without casting off entirely a lack of self confidence in dealing with unexpected problems or tricky situations. I was happy to be left to make many small decisions without the guidance of parents: to stand on my own two feet.

St George's was in many ways typical of the English public school of that era: deriving its mission from the muscular Christianity of Thomas Arnold's Rugby; confident of its mission to train its pupils to be leaders in the "civilisation" of the African people; and relying heavily on corporal punishment to maintain the standards of behaviour and steadfastness it set .

During my time St George's attracted two outstanding headmasters: Cecil Tugman, who was head from 1935 to 1944; and Philip Cuckow, who arrived in 1944 and was head until 1956. I came to know Tugman better, partly because of my early troubled period at the School. He had served with distinction in the Royal Artillery during the First World War until invalided out because of the effects of gas poisoning . Subsequently, he had many years experience as a teacher in Johannesburg, Grahamstown and Swaziland. He was described by one observer as: "strict, fair, a perfect gentleman, sportsman and friend", and as "a talented sportsman with a golden tongue".

He was also seen as "unashamedly highbrow... with a great depth of intellect" who often taught Latin entirely in that language. The boys, especially the more junior, regarded him as somewhat intimidating because of the high intellectual standards he set . My strong impression was of an essentially humane individual, who was eminently approachable, had a strong sense of humour, and wide interests outside the classroom (especially in drama). I have already noted his contribution to acquiring the Bloemendal site as a base for the boarders. He did much to support the development of sports and to improve communication with parents. But he was probably best remembered for what he did to raise the academic standards and standing of the School at Matriculation level.

Philip Cuckow was another who had taught at St Johns College in Johannesburg. He came to St Georges with a "no nonsense" reputation. He was described as "brisk and downright in his manner... often used sarcasm, and was wont to let out a barking shout when his patience failed him. But scrupulously fair with the boys who appreciated his honesty and candour". I will remember him most vividly for the sermon he delivered on President Roosevelt's death in 1945: a moving portrait of a man who had overcome the depression in America, drawn that country into the war, and above all given fresh hope to millions of Americans of a better life after war. Although I had departed South Africa before Cuckow's impact as head could be judged, I believe he introduced a more participative approach to decision making, setting up pupil committees to manage eg sporting competitions. He revived the School's magazine The Georgian and inaugurated a Development Fund to support key ambitions for improvements in facilities for pupils. He may be best remembered for presiding over the School's Centenary celebrations in 1948.

By mid-year 1945 the War in Europe was over; and it was time for expatriates to consider whether they would make their future in South Africa or return to complete their schooling in England. There was never any question that we would choose the latter course. For several months, Shirley and I were withdrawn from our respective schools whilst waiting for a suitable ship to carry us back to Liverpool. It was a dull period for us. But at length a ship became available; and we were on our way. The passage took an unusually long time to reach Liverpool: partly because the cargo ship needed to put into Freetown for several uncomfortably hot and humid days; and when she left Freetown fourteen stowaways were discovered in the cargo hold. We had to put into Dakar to put them ashore . Then, shortly before reaching Liverpool, a severe storm blew up in the Bay of Biscay; and the SS Tindareus was forced to shelter off Angelesea before proceeding to Liverpool. It was a tedious end to a somewhat tedious voyage. But at least we were back "home".

RETURN TO ENGLAND

We - Mummy, Shirley and I - arrived in Liverpool, after delays due to the storm in the Bay of Biscay and the western approaches, in the third week of September. As we set out on the taxi journey from the docks to Lime Street Station, we were shocked to see the devastation wrought by the German Luftwaffe bombers. The greater part of the residential buildings, as well as much of the harbour area, had been flattened; and little had been done - could have been done - to clear the damage, let alone rebuild the shattered houses. This brought home to me what I had been spared by my time in South Africa : you never know your good fortune!

When we reached our destination at my grandparents' home in Brookwood, Surrey (called "Dimbula" after one of the tea estates Poppy had managed during his time in Ceylon), we soon became aware of the tight rationing of food and many other basic necessities that was in force in Britain during the war years. The much quoted comedy line "Yes we have no bananas" summed up both the scarcity of food and the sturdy humour and resilience of much of the population. Britain was both derelict and broke; but people could at least congratulate themselves on surviving and achieving a remarkable victory over Germany. Moreover, the newly elected Labour Government, not at all welcomed by my grandparents, was optimistically setting about implementing the far reaching social and economic reforms for a "welfare state" recommended by Lord Beveridge's report "Social Insurance and Allied Services" (which was published in 1942). All this would slowly sink in as I settled into life in England.

My parents' plan was to send me to boarding school at Bedford, some fifty miles north of London. The reason for this choice, never fully explained, was partly that Poppy and several of his brothers had been pupils at the school in the late nineteenth century: I would be following a family tradition. Equally important, the tuition fees at

Bedford were reasonably modest compared with many other public schools. My parents had clearly ruled out the possibility that I might study at a local Surrey Grammar school, because they would have reckoned that my father would continue with his career in the Gold Coast until he reached the age of fifty. In that case, there would be no family home in Surrey; and I would therefore have to continue to be a boarder. Since there were no state boarding schools in Surrey my destination would have to be a private boarding school elsewhere.

Before I could claim a place at Bedford School there were two issues to be settled. I must satisfy Bedford that I would be worth a place; and that would entail taking exam papers set by the school. It was also necessary to establish whether Surrey County Council would meet part of the Bedford fees. Since I was too late to take the 11+ exam for admission to a Grammar School in Surrey , would the County be willing to meet the costs they would have incurred in placing me in one of their Grammar schools? I was despatched to a small Preparatory School in Hampshire to prepare for Bedford's entrance exams, whilst (I assume) my mother sorted out the answer to the second question with Surrey County Council.

At the end of the Michaelmas term at Harcourt School, I sat several exam papers set by Bedford School. Despite my almost total lack of any knowledge of Latin, I must have provided reasonable evidence of ability in other subjects to meet Bedford's standards for entry to their Lower School. As for Surrey's response to the question of fees, they generously accepted the case for meeting the fees at Bedford; and for the next six years treated me as though I had been placed in one of the state Grammar schools in the County. The way was clear for me to enrol at Bedford.

On a bleak winter's day in early January 1946, my mother delivered me to Farrar's, one of two boarding houses providing accommodation for boys of 11 to 13 years of age who lived too far away to attend Bedford's Lower School as dayboys. The Lower School had been established as a separate entity, with its own headmaster, in 1935. Its mission was to provide a rigorous academic regime to enable Bedford's Preparatory School pupils (in what was always known as the "Inky") to make the transition to the Upper School. It also served , after 1945, as an entry point for a significant number of state school pupils successful in the 11+ exam.

I was placed in form II 2, one step below the top class, to assess whether my grounding in South Africa equipped me to make the grade alongside pupils who had come through the "Inky" with good marks. (I was placed in a much lower class for Latin, where I had much ground to make up before I could sit alongside my II 2 peers).

Over the following three terms, I made sufficient progress to reach third place in my class of 20 boys; and to join them in the same class for Latin. My reports (still in my possession) indicated marked strengths in English, History and French, but more modest achievement in mathematics: a pattern that would recur as I moved (in 1947) into the top class for 13 year old entrants to the Upper School .

It is not my progress in the classroom that stays in my mind when I reflect on my time in the Lower School - nor my success on the playing field (where I made some impact as a centre and fly half on the rugby field, and scored some useful runs on the cricket pitch). My sharpest memories are of two events that took place at Farrar's.

The first of these was the severe winter weather that struck the whole country at the beginning of 1947, and which held us in its grip through to the end of February. Masses of snow fell in January; and we boarders enjoyed the experience of tobogganing down Clapham Hill - and just about getting off before our toboggan landed in the ditch at the bottom of the slope. The local pond froze solidly enough to take the weight of small boys. Here I was not so lucky. I fell heavily in racing and sliding over the ice, and had to have stitches inserted under my eyebrow.

What I chiefly recall, however,w as not the winter sport, but the acute fuel crisis that hit the country as coal stocks became exhausted as a result of the increased demand. It was bitterly cold outside, and it was difficult indoors to keep the chill at bay. There has not since been a cold spell to rival that of 1947!

My second, and sadder, memory is of the occasion when my housemaster came up to our dormitory, and beckoned me to accompany him to his study. I recall vividly his bent finger silently pointing the way for me. When I was seated, Mr Sutcliffe asked when I had last seen my father. He then told me that Daddy had died a few days previously of heart failure brought on by very high blood pressure . I was shocked and numbed by this news: so numbed that I did not burst into tears (as Mr Sutcliffe no doubt expected). He was of course very sympathetic and gentle. He steered the conversation to my memories of my father; and of our family circumstances. He promised to inform the Lower School headmaster what had happened; and doubtless passed word to some of my fellow boarders. The general tone of the conversation was to encourage me to try to continue with my normal routine as far as possible: people would make allowances if my school work suffered, but it was better to keep going as normal.

When I reflected on Daddy's passing, I acknowledged that I had been aware of the deterioration of his health. He had had "turns" during the course of our spring holiday the previous year. I knew that he had retired from his post in Achimota on ill health grounds, and returned to England to get better medical attention. But I had no inkling of the seriousness of his condition; and my mother and family evidently thought it wiser to withhold from me information of his doctor's assessment. Daddy died on 13 March, the day before my thirteenth birthday; so they could be excused waiting a few days before I was told of his death. But I was, less excusably, left in the dark about the arrangements for his cremation at the Woking Crematorium. I had no opportunity to say goodbye!

Mummy wrote to me some days after my interview with Mr Sutcliffe to commiserate with me about Daddy's death. The burden of her letter was: "Daddy would have been an invalid if he had survived; and you know how he would have hated that". She consistently avoided any show of grief; and indeed any discussion of his life or his death. Her general attitude was that we must get on with our lives and not mope. To discuss any details of their life together was an indulgence best avoided. Over the years she adopted this coping strategy - to the extent that Shirley and I felt inhibited about seeking more information about Daddy's life and work. After all these years, I still feel slightly deprived of our "birthright". If we could not have our father live on with us, could we not at least be allowed some memories of him: for example of his contribution to the building of Achimota; how he coped with the pressures from the army's demands for suitable accommodation on the Achimota compound; and his relations with his Scottish family.? Did Mummy's vow of silence really help her to come to terms with her loss? I shall now never know! What I do know is that I continued to regret not knowing my father better.

At the end of my time at Farrar's and in the Lower School, having successfully negotiated the Common Entrance exams, I was "posted" in September 1947 to Sanderson's, one of five boarding houses for boys in the Upper School. The house accommodated, as far as I recall, around forty boys. I was one of eight of the most junior thirteen year-olds. The housemaster was a bachelor, Harry Mackay, who taught French and History to the Remove classes (14/15 year olds) in a highly idiosyncratic style which was very amusing and effective. He ran the house with a relatively light touch, leaving much of the disciplinary matters to the senior boys (the house monitors).

None of Bedford's boarding houses had been built for the purpose of accommodating 40 or so boys. Sanderson's was probably typical: originally a residence for a substantial family and its servants, and acquired by the school to meet the growing demand for boarding accommodation. It comprised four dormitories and a large common room which served as dining room, prep room for home work, a space for some leisure pursuits, lockers for books and other personal items - and was the space where the monitors administered corporal punishment! There were fairly primitive showering and changing facilities; and a single study for the head of the house. Outside were a nissen hut for table tennis and billiards, and a lawn tennis court. Shortage of funds had prevented much improvement in facilities before the war intervened to make that impossible. It was a bleak environment to serve as "home" for the next five years.

A contemporary of mine at Sanderon's, Michael De-la-Noy, who was commissioned by the School Governors to write the official history of Bedford School in 1999, included in that history an unpublished "fragment of a memoir" by a boy who recorded his impressions of life at Sanderson's in the late forties. It reads as follows:

"Hunger, cold and lack of privacy are my abiding memories of school. We slept in unheated dormitories with all the windows open, under two thin ex-army blankets. Without threepenny portions of chips, tipped into cone-shaped paper packets through which fat oozed on to your fingers and then on to your bicycle handlebars, I doubt whether I should have survived the long hours between lunch and tea. For warmth we huddled, when the monitors allowed us to, in front of one intermittent coal fire in the common room, and when we were chucked out of there so that tables could be laid for meals, we congregated in the changing rooms, where at least the hot water pipes provided some degree of comfort."

"There was only one study at Sanderson's... The rest of us slept, worked and ate perpetually surrounded by the noise, distraction and intrusion of forty other boys, towards whom we were largely indifferent or actively hostile. I have always thought it particularly hard on anyone of my generation sent to prison who had not first experienced a public school's inadequate and often uneatable food, mindless violence, carefully arranged discomfort, adherence to petty rules and inadequate sanitary arrangements [which] were all endemic in my day. Prison should hold few terrors for any Old Bedfordian boarders over fifty."

I strongly suspect that Michael was himself the author of this tirade. It bears all the hallmarks of his characteristic journalistic style! It is colourful, trenchant and occasionally inaccurate. Nonetheless I and my contemporaries would corroborate most of the points this "anonymous" writer makes. And one could add that the lack of any female presence made the scene the more dreary!

The Bedford School of my time (I entered the Upper School in 1948 and left it in July 1952 to serve the statutory two years as a national serviceman) was not a pathfinder among the British public schools. It held broadly to the late nineteenth century traditions established, most notably, by Thomas Arnold's Rugby . The key elements of this tradition were: the "fagging system"; compulsory religion and games; the monitorial system; and extensive use of the cane to enforce discipline - and, of course, no contact with girls!

Several headmasters had made some attempt to regulate or soften the use of the cane - or to justify its use. One had insisted that there should be a limit of three "cuts"; another proposed that only masters be permitted to use the cane. The head during my time at Bedford, Humfrey Grose-Hodge, had argued that " the object of caning is to compel a boy's attention, to impress on him that his fault is serious and to break down his obduracy". Its value, he suggested, depended less on the deterrent effect of flogging, more on what is said to the boy afterwards! In my experience - both as victim and,on only one occasion, as administrator of corporal punishment, the most valid and important criticism of caning at Bedford was that it was largely decided and administered by senior boys, with remarkably little effective supervision or checks by the headmaster or housemasters.

The "fagging system", under which the most junior boys carried out diverse menial tasks for the head of the boarding house, was still in operation in my time. Despite the obvious risks of exploitation and abuse, and the demeaning character, there was little challenge to the institution, which was credited with being a useful way of educating the younger members of the boarding house in their duty of service to the community.

The school had made laudable attempts to widen the academic syllabus to include science subjects and languages other than Latin and Greek; but the core of teaching was the classics and English.

The work of the school was carried out not in the boarding houses but in the Victorian Gothic building , opened in 1891 by the Duke of Bedford ,that was designed to provide instruction for nearly 1000 pupils (the majority of them dayboys). This impressive red brick edifice had a very large (over 100 feet long) great hall where the Upper School assembled for most formal occasions; and two tiers of galleries , surrounded by over 40 classrooms. The building looked out over extensive playing fields spread over about five hectares of land.

The opening of the main school building was the culmination of an extraordinary growth in demand for places for pupils, and of a growing reputation, in the latter half of the nineteenth century, especially during the headmastership of James Surtees Philpott (from 1875 to 1903). During this period the school attracted many pupils whose parents had made their careers in Britain's imperial outposts or in the military that won or protected these overseas territories. Many came to live in Bedford just to take advantage of the education the school provided. My grandfather's family was an example of this.

This growth in school numbers (which at one point made the school one of the three or four largest public schools) was a far cry from the relative handful of "poor scholars" whose education at the time the school was founded in 1552 was funded largely by rents from London properties bequeathed to the Bedford Corporation by Sir William Harper in 1566. Like many foundations in the reign of Edward VI, the motivation to establish a grammar school at Bedford was prompted by the dissolution of the monasteries, which deprived the town of the teaching establishment previously run by monks. It might be said that the prominent influence of the public schools in succeeding centuries owed much to the destruction of the monasteries.

A schoolboy's recall of his schooldays is usually greatly influenced by the characters of the masters who taught him. I remember two very different men who guided my footsteps. GCF Mead (always remembered as "Pussy" Mead) was the form master who steered me through the year leading to the School Certificate exams in 1949. He was a bachelor without any of the "quirks" that often characterise schoolmasters. He was quiet, patient, observant and dedicated, but with a marked ability to enhance one's appreciation of the English language: its grammar, poetry, drama and idiosyncracies. I learned more about how the language "worked", and how to convey ideas simply and economically, in that year than at any time before or since.

Even more influential was John Eyre, who was my form master and history teacher in my last two years. He has been described by Paddy Ashdown, who studied under Eyre some years after I did, as "a tall gaunt man with lanky hair who came across as a rebel... I remember wondering why on earth he came to teach at a place like Bedford". Eyre was an ex-public schoolboy (at Wellington), who had become radicalised during his time as an officer in the army during the Second World War. He was an intellectual, who made no attempt to conceal his scorn for those he judged woolly or misguided. He was a committed member of the Labour Party in a school that leaned pretty much to the right. And he had a passion for pushing his pupils to reconsider many of the received views about episodes in British and European history. I recall he opened my eyes to the virtues of

Thomas Cromwell, Henry VIII's "enforcer". He encouraged me to stand as the Labour candidate in the mock election held by the school in 1951 (I got precious few votes!). Most importantly, John Eyre persuaded me that I had it within my capacity to win a scholarship to Oxford or Cambridge. (he would be disappointed here too, as I shall explain in a later chapter!).

My progress during these formative years, through to School Certificate and on to A Level exams, was steady rather than spectacular. I would probably have been described as intelligent and conscientious rather than brilliant; and , as far as games were concerned, enthusiastic rather than outstanding (Third XV at rugby and Third XI at cricket). Quite early on it was predicted that I should specialise after School Certificate in History and English; and I readily concurred in that assessment. From the moment I passed the School Certificate exams with Credits in most subjects and distinctions in History and English Literature, my course was set.

I entered the History Sixth, and began to make a mark academically. I won the History Essay prize for a piece on my ancestor, John Winthrop (based largely, I admit, on the magisterial two-volume biography by Robert Winthrop!). I also won the school's essay prize (on the set theme of "The Elizabethan Era") for a somewhat pedestrian account of the history of the reign of Elizabeth I. (I ignored the temptation to speculate on the reign of Elizabeth II, which began in 1952!). I also won the Form Prize that year. It was an abridged and prudishly edited version of DH Lawrence's novel, "Lady Chatterley's Lover ", delivered into my hands on Speech Day 1952 by Princess Margaret (I did not then appreciate the irony of this choice: the affair of Princess Margaret and Peter Townsend had yet to become public knowledge!).

Outside the classroom I achieved my main ambition of being appointed one of the school's monitors, and also became head of Sanderson's. The monitors had a large measure of responsibility for running school clubs and societies, for organising games, and for maintaining discipline. We had the privilege of wearing brown shoes; and we wielded a cane at school assembly as a symbol of our authority. But it was this custom that led to the most unfortunate incident of my career at Bedford.

It happened at the end of the Michaelmas term of 1951. As the monitors gathered in their room before the morning assembly, we discovered that someone had removed the canes from every locker. We were f orced to proceed into the Great Hall without this badge of authority. It was my turn that morning to prepare the grand piano for the playing of the appointed hymn by the Director of Music, Dr Probert Jones. Imagine my horror, when I r aised the piano lid , I found a dozen or so canes laid neatly across the piano strings!

I froze. I could not bring myself to do the obvious thing: pick up the canes and return quickly to my seat. After pondering the situation for a few moments, I concluded that the best course would be to let the head boy know what I had found: let him decide what should be done. However, by the time that I had reported to the head boy, the Headmaster , Clarence Seaman, and Dr Probert Jones were already advancing to their places on the platform. The inevitable happened: as the first notes of the hymn were struck, there was nothing but a dull thud! . Whilst the pupils themselves could scarcely contain their laughter, the Head was furious and the Director of Music no doubt felt humiliated. The body of monitors was mightily embarrassed: they must have felt that they had let down the (newly appointed) Headmaster, and given him the impression that this was a joke organised by the monitors to make him look silly. I could only wish that the floor would open up to provide a means of abject retreat.

In the years since this incident, when I have reflected uncomfortably on my failure of nerve and inability to confront boldly an awkward situation, I have also wondered whether, in a small way, I may have influenced the decision of the Headmaster to resign from his post after an unusually short period at Bedford. He had taught classics at Bedford before the War, but was certainly never entirely happy with the culture of Bedford School. This incident may have helped to confirm his doubts? He moved to become Headmaster of Christ's Hospital in 1955.

It would be an exaggeration to suggest that this incident cast a blight on my final few months at Bedford. For one thing, the Christmas break, which followed immediately afterwards, gave time for most of the people involved to forget the episode. For me, however, it remained in my mind for years as a warning and a challenge: a warning of the unhappy consequences of failing to confront problems directly and promptly; and a challenge to develop the character to do so.

I said goodbye to Bedford at the end of the summer term of 1952. I cannot say that I was sad to leave behind my schooldays. I did not feel that I had achieved as much as I could and should have done. I had many regrets: I wished I had read much more widely; my musical education was largely limited to the hymns we sang ; I had made very few close friends; and I had virtually no contacts with girls from Bedford High school! These omissions were largely my own fault. But the school did little to lead me to address them. I was, as it struck me in later years, not sufficiently mature - intellectually, emotionally and socially - to seize or create the opportunities to progress as I would have wished. For these reasons I could never believe that my schooldays would prove to be "the happiest days of my life".

UP TO CAMBRIDGE

Ever since I had moved into the Sixth Form I expected that I would proceed to university to study history on completion of my time at Bedford. In those far off days, that usually meant a choice between Oxford and Cambridge. Though there were in truth a number of excellent alternatives to Oxbridge, most of my contemporaries tended to think first about which Oxbridge college might be suitable for them rather than to consider other universities. In my case, my choice of Cambridge - and in particular of Pembroke College - was influenced by the fact that my headmaster at Bedford, Humfrey Grose-Hodge, was a close friend of the Master of Pembroke, Sir Sidney Roberts. I suspect that my Form Master, John Eyre, must have discussed my prospects with the headmaster; and that the latter may have "had a word" with his old friend. At all events, on a sunny afternoon in the early summer of 1951, and shortly before my A level exams, I was ushered into the rooms in Pembroke College of Mr WA (Tony) Camps, the Senior Tutor, to discuss my request to enrol in the College.

Tony Camps was the Tutor largely responsible for selecting students for the College. In this position - and later, when he became Master - he had a significant influence on the character of the College through the decisions he had to take on enrolments. He was, as I later learned, widely trusted and respected, as a wise and generous spirit, anxious to extend the intake of students from less well known and prestigious schools, and ready to take a risk on people with less than glowing academic credentials.

My interview with Mr Camps, after initial pleasantries, began with a question of logic, which I failed to answer convincingly. I was then taken on a relaxed stroll through the College gardens, then at their most beautiful, while Camps taxed me with questions about my family, my course at Bedford and my hopes for Cambridge. He was kindly - not to say indulgent - but I felt that I had not advanced my claims for a place at the College. I was therefore surprised and delighted to receive a letter the following day offering me a place, subject to confirmation in the light of the results of my A level exams. This decision was subsequently confirmed when I received a decent A level outcome and achieved reasonable marks at the Scholarship exams at the College (which I sat shortly before Christmas 1951, though I was not offered a Scholarship!).

So my course was set - but I had first to do my two years' national service before going up to Cambridge.

I had chosen to enlist in the Navy, with the objective of becoming a Russian interpreter. At a time of increasing international tension, both in the middle east and on the Korean peninsular, the Navy had decided to increase its recruitment of national servicemen, and had identified a particular requirement for people who were adapt at Russian. Why not me? In the event, I was not selected for training as an Interpreter (the Navy was already having second thoughts about the intake of would-be interpreters, and was cutting back!). But the Navy were happy to appoint me to a post on the education side . Soon after I joined up, however,and began the basic training undertaken by all new recruits, I discovered there were opportunities to undergo officer training for service afloat. This appealed much more than educating navy personnel. I therefore embarked on a course for (so called) Upperyardsmen designed to prepare suitably equipped young men for service as Midshipmen on ships of the fleet. Most of my time as a national serviceman was therefore spent at sea (or as much at sea as the Navy could afford!)

My first appointment as a Midshipman was to HMS Illustrious, an aircraft carrier whose main mission was to train pilots of the Naval Air Service, especially in the hazardous business of flying on and off flight decks in heavy seas. I had no part in the flying: my main duties were assisting more senior officers in sailing the ship to various ports around the British Isles which offered a range of tests for the flyers.

My most vividly remembered experience of this time was navigating a Motor Fishing Vessel, which was an auxiliary tender to the carrier, through the Irish Sea to its destination in Cornwall. I have never been so prostrated by seasickness as on that voyage through a turbulent ocean; and my contribution to accurate navigation was negligible!

My second appointment was to a considerably smaller vessel: a frigate, HMS Redpoll, engaged in training prospective navigation officers in the specialist skills of directing ships on an efficient and safe course. The complement of officers was small, and as a Midshipman I had much more responsibility for managing the crew and steering the ship. My captain was an expert in terrestrial navigation and setting course by sun and stars; but he was less proficient in the task of man-management or the handling of a ship in rough weather conditions. I could not rescue him from a singularly unfortunate attempt to manoeuvre his ship alongside a much larger Navy vessel in a heavy cross wind. Much damage was done to both ships - and, I guess, to my captain's reputation!

Though I enjoyed my seagoing experience, and learned a lot about managing seamen and supporting more senior officers, I was never tempted to make the Navy a career. I was more than happy to complete my compulsory two year stint and revert to the course already decided-- and make my way back to Cambridge.

The Cambridge I joined in the autumn of 1954 had only recently emerged from the task of educating a substantial number of students returning after the Second World War to c omplete their university courses or to take up opportunities for university education they had had to defer for war service(the so called "warriors"). My contemporaries were, in a sense, the vanguard of the post- war generation. Few of us had been involved in battle zones; but the majority had done national service and come up in their early twenties, older and, presumably, more mature than the average pre-war undergraduates (arguably, one of the benefits of compulsory military service!). The dominance of public (that is private) schools and the best known grammar schools was just as pronounced as ever; and the student body was overwhelmingly male (Pembroke College would not admit women until the 1980s!). The great expansion of university education , following the Robbins Report, would not come until the 1960s. We were an in-between generation (representing little more than 5% of the school leaver population) before the gates of academe opened much wider to the population of eighteen year- olds and a broader range of schools. Most of us were fortunate to have been awarded County Scholarships which provided finance to cover much of the living costs of the university course (and there was no question of our meeting tuition fees!). We were also lucky to enjoy the prospect of emerging on to a buoyant labour market at the end of our university course (since graduates were a scarce commodity).

On a bright autumn day in October 1954, I passed the threshold of Pembroke College, there to be accosted by the senior Porter, the official guardian of the College entrance gate. He informed me that I was to be allocated rooms in the most recently constructed building at the far end of the College estate; and wished me luck!

As I made my way there, I was struck by the fact that the layout and architecture of the College did not follow the traditional "cloistered" arrangement of closed courtyards typical of colleges established in the late middle ages (as Pembroke had been). Most of the residential blocks were set at the edge of the College precinct, looking out mainly on the lawns and gardens, which were one of the attractive features of the College. This "openness", I was told, reflected the relatively open and relaxed style of the College community as a whole.

The residential block to which I was directed was not an architectural splendour! It was solid and serviceable rather than elegant and stylish; and it provided the minimum of washing , bathing and cooking facilities (baths were to be found several blocks away and involved often a decidedly chilly walk across several blocks to get a warm dip!).

However, the newish building was a useful addition to the College estate and enabled the College to offer all newcomers the possibility of spending their first year in College rather than in "digs" in remote parts of Cambridge: a great benefit.

Once settled in our rooms, and having exchanged greetings with other newcomers, it was time to arrange to meet the key Fellows who would be guiding and supervising our activities: Bill Hutton was to be the Tutor with broadly pastoral and general , rather than academic, responsibilities for our welfare. This Tutor role was somewhat undeveloped in my time; in practice I saw little of Mr Hutton, and never felt the need to consult him on financial, health or welfare matters - partly because he had too wide a range of duties in managing the college estate to devote much attention to pastoral issues.

My Director of Studies was David Joslin. It was his role to ensure that my academic work was guided, supervised and challenged in ways that enabled me to make the most of the opportunities that Cambridge had to offer - and of course to produce written work that prepared me for the Tripos exams at the end of my second and third years. Supervisions with him were a key part of my weekly commitments in my first year. Thereafter it was often necessary for another Fellow to cover special subjects. But Joslin was always approachable, friendly and wise in the encouragement he provided.

The other "character" who would prove a valuable counsellor to those in trouble was Rev Meredith Dewey. He not only gave ready help to those with emotional or spiritual problems, and led services in the Wren Chapel, but served delicious cucumber sandwiches.

These three personalities —and Tony Camps--typified the informal, supportive and readily accessible character of the Pembroke Fellowship in my time.

One could describe the education we gained as supported on three legs of the academic "Tripod" (which gave its name to the Tripos exams): University lectures; one-to-one supervisions of written work under the guidance (usually) of the College directors of studies for the relevant subject; and study in one of the university libraries. In my experience, most undergraduates tended to give less prominence to formal lectures, and to rely more on their directors of studies and on private reading.

However, a large number of first year historians were glad to sit at the feet of lecturers such as John Saltmarsh, whose series on economic history was felt by many to be an essential introduction to the history Tripos. In his carefully modulated and precise high-pitched voice, and reading from lecture notes honed over many years, Saltmarsh took us through aspects of medieval economic history which few of us had confronted at school. His lectures were a demonstration of the virtues of the traditional lecture ; but offered no opportunity to interrupt to ask questions or challenge assertions, which are an equally valuable aspect of learning.

Weekly supervisions of prescribed written work were generally regarded as an essential means of keeping students on their mettle. My first experience of this discipline was when I was set to write an essay during my first week on Horatio Nelson, by a Fellow who had, like me, experience of serving in the Royal Navy. It was not a happy experience. In my two years service in the Navy I had written virtually no passages longer than brief entries in my Midshipman's log book. I had forgotten how to organise an essay; and found it difficult to focus on essential detail or to think through coherently what aspect of Nelson's career deserved analysis. As I read, increasingly uncomfortably, my inept offering, my supervisor, Mr Dickinson, lay almost prone in front of his gas fire, half asleep, appearing to take little interest in my efforts. He woke up to ask what significance Nelson had to the future of the Navy; to which I offered in reply nothing of consequence! It was a salutary experience, from which (I hoped) I would learn.

Fortunately, my director of studies, David Joslin, subsequently took me in hand. A series of sessions with him over the following year gave me more confidence in compiling essays, and much more satisfaction from discussion and argument. He justified the emphasis that Cambridge gave to the benefits of well organised supervisions. But I believe that the experience of supervisions could have been improved by the involvement of several fellow students in the debate. That conviction was reinforced when, in my final year, Joslin arranged a discussion with several students pursuing the same special subject (all of us feeling let down by the quality of the formal lectures we had attended). This proved one of the most satisfying learning experiences of my time at Cambridge.

The university and history libraries were an essential resource for all students; and it was agreeable to bury oneself comfortably for an afternoon's browsing among the massive collections of documents-- before repairing to one's rooms for tea and crumpets from Fitzbillie's, the outstanding patisserie in Cambridge. I have to confess, however, that my most rewarding period of research was in the British Museum library during my final Christmas vacation. There, in the famous round reading room where Karl Marx had studied for his Commmunist Manifesto, I spent a solid two weeks digging up documents about the Boxer Rebellion, my special subject in my third year. This experience gave me a much better appreciation of what is required of the serious historian.

Study for a degree was, of course, only a part of one's engagement with university life : there was an enormous range of activities, societies, entertainment and social contacts that readily took possession of students' time and energy. The first year could easily be largely taken up with making choices about what to focus on - and the second and third years with regrets about those choices! I came up with no set plan. But I found quite early that I was drawn to take a particular interest in, and commitment to, international relations. This was initially spurred by a project to set up a branch of the United Nations

Association to bring together both members of the university and those enrolled in the three language schools for foreign students which had been set up in Cambridge.

The main reason for this initiative was to encourage more contact between university students and the considerable number of foreign students not enrolled in the university. The latter were not entitled to join, or at least not welcomed by, university societies such as Cambridge University United Nations Association (CUUNA). Since a large proportion of foreign students were women they would help to even out the gender imbalance within the university student population - with benefits all round .

I was drawn into this project by Humfrey Todd, a fellow first year history student at Pembroke, whose father was Secretary of the Cambridge City UNA and who doubtless wished to help overseas students engage with the university in discussions on international matters. Humfrey and I, with several other Pembroke historians (notably Brian Corkery and Reg Evers) set about selling this project to the three language schools. They greeted the idea with enthusiasm. We enlisted a number of students from these schools in a small informal group to help market the proposed UNA branch within the three schools and in Cambridge colleges ; and to organise a programme of social activities and talks etc which might generate interest in some of the problems that beset international relations.

Not surprisingly we stirred up a good deal of interest and enthusiasm among overseas students, and within several colleges. We soon had over fifty members of the fledgeling association; and a programme of events for the Christmas term , culminating in a very successful social gathering, with entertainment provided by a group of Norwegians singing a selection of folk songs. Over the remainder of the academic year we became one of the most successful bodies linking the University and the non-university populations.

For me, one of the major benefits was to establish friendships with a number of overseas students, especially females, who helped to overcome my shyness and inhibitions about dating young women! One of them particularly attracted my attention: Nina Torbjornsen, a Norwegian girl a little younger than I, but a great deal more mature and self-confident, with an outgoing manner and an enjoyment of life. Over the months before Nina returned to her native Oslo, we saw a lot of one another. I introduced her to Gilbert and Sullivan and other British institutions; and she was my partner at the dinner dance in London celebrating my 21st birthday. More important ,we spent many hours discussing the issues of the day over late night coffees; and I began to acquire some understanding and appreciation of the Scandinavian approach to social and political problems. Though there was no question of a "romantic" association, we came to value a friendship without hang-ups; and we were determined to maintain friendly contact after Nina returned to Norway (and we kept that promise for nearly fifty years!).

One example of the impact and attraction of our Association was a coffee party which Reg Evers and I hosted at our digs in October 1955, at the beginning of our second academic year. We let it be known in the language schools that we would welcome to our informal party any students who would be interested in joining the United Nations Association. We expected a small handful would make their way out to our digs, some distance from the centre of Cambridge. In the event, more than twenty appeared! Our good-hearted landlady retreated to her bedroom, and allowed us to take over her living room and Kitchen to accommodate this multitude. I do not recall how we coped with the demand for coffee and biscuits. But the gathering generated lively conversation and a number of useful contacts.

Three individuals attracted my attention. Sylvia Plath had just arrived in Cambridge on a Fulbright Scholarship, and had been invited to the party by my friend Brian Corkery. We knew nothing of her talents as a poet - and she had not then entered into the intense relationship with Ted Hughes which later attracted much attention - but she made an engaging and instructive contribution to our conversation. Berit Ohlson and Lionella Orlandini had just embarked on a course at the Davies's School and become close friends. They were an attractive duo, and would come to play a major part in the lives of Humfrey Todd and myself: as I shall record in my next Chapter.

One consequence of the success of our Association in attracting considerable support among the body of foreign students was the recognition by CUUNA that they were missing a trick. Surely they should also be grasping the opportunity to embrace and welcome into membership the students from outside the University whom we had been recruiting? Before long, the CUUNA Committee, in discussion with Humfrey and myself, decided they would take the step of offering membership to these students; and at the same time coopted me to their Committee. In effect, CUUNA took over the role we had been playing, and enabled the overseas students to enjoy the benefits that had previously been closed to them (and greatly expanded CUUNA's membership to over 800, making it one of the largest and most prominent of University societies).

This move had the result that, in my last year or so, I became an active member of the CUUNA Committee. I was elected Treasurer and, in due course, sought election as Chairman. I lost that contest by only two votes. This may have been a blessing in disguise, since I had several other commitments to occupy me intensively in the run up to Finals; and I could ill afford the time to manage the CUUNA committee as well. I did, however, lead a study group set up by CUUNA to consider the future role of the United Nations in the conflict-ridden world of the late 1950s. In due course, we published a short pamphlet drawing attention to the value of efforts of UN agencies (WHO, UNESCO, ILO etc) in assisting the resolution of eg health and labour problems which undermined the development of many countries. I also represented the University at the annual conference of the United Nations Student Association, held at Durham at the end of 1956.

Like many others, I was shaken by the two international crises that took place in autumn 1956: the Suez war and the Hungarian uprising. Both these events awakened among Cambridge students a greater degree of indignation and political involvement than anything else in that decade. We were shamed by the duplicity of Prime Minister Anthony Eden in his pursuit of his vendetta against Egypt's President Nasser. At an angry debate at the Cambridge Union, the President of the union felt driven to say: "I am sorry at this time I belong to the British nation. We have kicked the United Nations in the guts."

There was no part that students could realistically play in securing the retreat from Suez by British and French troops. By contrast, many of us were very active in trying to support the Hungarians in their resistance to the Russian invasion of that country - and helping those who sought refuge in other countries after they had fled Hungary. A number of my friends set out for Vienna in the hope of lending support to the Hungarian "rebels". For my part, I took the advice of the Austrian authorities that our best course was to concentrate our efforts at home on raising as much money as possible to send via various aid agencies to relieve the distress of Hungarian refugees. I recall organising a lorry load of clothing and other needed items to be dispatched to Vienna.

Towards the end of my time at Cambridge, as I began to form plans for the future, I became more and more interested in the possibility of further study rather than looking for employment on completion of my degree course. There were two strands to my thinking. First, I was excited by the prospect of studying in the USA. And, second, I was increasingly persuaded of the importance of improving the culture of industrial relations in British industry. I had a number of American friends who encouraged the first of these objectives. Moreover, I soon discovered that some US universities had developed considerable strengths in the field of industrial relations, whereas in Britain this subject had been largely neglected. I therefore began to explore options for studying industrial sociology in the United States.

Harvard was, I hoped, a good place to start my search. My Winthrop connections would perhaps "open a few doors"?

Unhappily, Harvard were not sufficiently impressed - or financed - to offer me a place. I therefore explored two other possibilities: Wisconsin State University, which had a good academic reputation for research in industrial sociology; and the recently established New York School of Industrial and Labor Relations located at Cornell University. This latter school set great store, I was advised, by its close and influential contacts with industry. Early in 1957 I heard from Cornell that they would offer me a place on a course leading to the qualification of Master of Industrial and Labor Relations(MILR). They could not however, offer me a grant to cover the cost of tuition or living expenses.

At this point, I discovered that NATO were offering a number of scholarships for study at American Universities to students from member nations. I duly applied; and was interviewed for one of these opportunities. Though supported by the UK government, I was turned down when applications from other countries were considered. My remaining hope was to attract finance from a private source. My dear friend Lord Charles Lyle(Uncle Charles, who had been a close friend of the family for many years and was almost a guardian to me after my father's death) was happy to step in to help. I therefore accepted the offer from Cornell; and began my preparations for travel to America in the autumn of 1957.

My preoccupations with international and industrial issues did not stand in the way of an often hectic and intense social "whirl". The College system at Cambridge greatly encouraged the development of firm and lasting friendships. One often dropped in on fellow students living in adjacent or nearby rooms for a chat, only to end up in lively discourse into the small hours: lubricated by tea or coffee, or something stronger. These contacts often led to expeditions to wider locations, as the friendships deepened. In my case, I recall joining up with Richard Dickenson - also an historian - for a three week camping holiday in Norway; and with Peter Duppa-Miller, a chemical engineer, for a hitch-hiking holiday in France and Spain, which concluded with an uncomfortable ride in a horse-box on the last leg of our journey to Calais.

Nearer to hand, Cambridge offered an enormous range of events, performances, debates and entertainment which could easily fill ones diary, and distract from academic commitments. The only constraints, apart from supervisions, were the expectation that one ate dinner in Hall; that one wear a gown after dark; and that one must return to College by 11 pm after a night out (and that no women should be found in College after that hour!). In practice I sometimes climbed back to my rooms in College over a two metre iron gate when the main entrance to the College shut at 11. And there were many occasions when I laboured through the small hours to complete an essay for a supervision the following morning.

In the months leading up to my Final exams in May 1957, I became more diligent in preparing for this crucial test. In the first part of the Tripos, I had been awarded a II.1 mark; and I hoped to do no worse in my Finals. I did not regard my prospects of achieving a First as good; but I did not wish to rule out that possibility by omitting a last spurt in my revision. In the end, however, after three days of intense effort in the examination hall, I had to accept that a II.1 was the likely outcome. And so it proved!

My last sight of Cambridge as an undergraduate was at the graduation ceremony in the Senate House, where those who had just passed their final exams bowed before the Chancellor of the University, who mumbled some Latin pieties over us in awarding us our degrees. This ceremony was attended by my mother and Aunt Barbara, and by Uncle Charles, who had driven me up to Cambridge from Pirbright for the occasion. I hoped they felt happy that I had not fallen back from my Part I mark - as had three of my close friends: Humphrey and Reg obtained II.2 awards, and Brian a Third. (Richard Dickenson was unwell at the time of the Finals; and was awarded what was called an "Aegrotat": that is an unclassified Degree). I was glad they wished to see me receive my degree.

How did I feel about my time at Cambridge? At the time, I noted in a letter to Berit Ohlson that "Cambridge has had a far greater influence on me than anything else can ever have done in helping me to see and set things in their true perspective, and enabling me to meet so many challenging and stimulating people". But I acknowledged that it was too early to judge what Cambridge meant to me. There was, however, no doubt in my mind that it was the most stimulating period of my life - and the most valuable learning experience. I don't think I made quite the advance in academic achievement I hoped for. I did not explore the subjects and issues that the syllabus covered with the critical quality they deserved. But the many-sided opportunities available at Cambridge - within the College and beyond - gave me the chance to develop my capacities and interests in many other ways. I could not ask for more!

A BURGEONING ROMANCE

In the months following the extraordinarily crowded coffee party of late October 1955, I saw no more of Sylvia Plath. She had other affairs to attend to! But I did meet up with Berit and Lionella on a handful of occasions at (as far as I recall) events organised by the United Nations Association. They seemed an inseparable pair: Lionella very dependant on the friendship to help her both with the language and with the mysteries of life in England. I recall, in particular, dancing with Berit to the strains of "Arrivederci Roma", a popular melody sweeping the country. I also recall attending a lecture with Berit: while I concentrated my attention on the substance of the lecture, she listened to the music of Mozart being played in the room above. We enjoyed the contrast of preferences!

Although I saw a good deal of Berit in the run up to Christmas, and felt comfortable in her company, we would have described our relationship as a warm friendship rather than anything more serious. In the early months of 1956, however, everything changed. As Berit herself records in a letter of 29 May, sent from Bromma soon after her return to Sweden: "I remember so well when I first realised what you meant - or could mean-- to me." She had come to tea at my digs in Hurst Park Avenue; and I had offered to walk her home. "You helped me to put my scarf on and I was surprised at my strong feelings and... when we walked home we took each other's hands of some internal mutual feeling that no one can explain. It's strange but I think that all our fundamental interests and viewpoints show the same direction".

I recall this occasion as if it were yesterday - and had much the same sense of surprise and delight. As we embraced in the darkened street, it struck me that this was what the French call a "coup de foudre"! A blow of fate. Though I could not then say it was love, I felt an overwhelming conviction at that moment that we must strive to deepen our relationship to test whether we wanted to make a life together. I believed Berit felt much the same.

What had changed? And why? One factor was certainly that I was emerging from a sadly unsatisfying relationship with a girl I had met, and become close to, in a summer vacation job picking hops on the Guinness farm in Sussex. Far more important was my growing recognition of Berit's qualities and character. She was utterly honest and trustworthy: she could no more lie than light a moonbeam! She was very perceptive about people, but generous and fairminded in her judgements about them. Her qualities of loyalty were well demonstrated in her support for Lionella. She had, to an unusual degree, a moral courage which enabled her to confront difficult issues directly and honestly. But, above all, she had great warmth, and a keen sense of fun. The fact that she was Swedish also counted with me: I had come to appreciate something of the admirable openness and egalitarian character of Sweden - as well as the attractions of their blond young women!

Over the next four months - before Berit was to return to Sweden to assist in the equestrian Olympic games held that summer in Stockholm - we became very close. Though I was much taken up with work for the first part of the Tripos, and with commitments on the CUUNA committee, and Berit had an au pair job with a local family, we were able to spend much time together: for example a trip to Stratford to see a performance of Hamlet. By Easter, I felt sufficiently sure of my feelings to invite Berit to spend the Easter weekend at my home in Pirbright. This gave her the chance to meet my mother and aunt and my sister Shirley - and perhaps to gain an insight into the family she might choose to join?

The occasion I remember most clearly, however, was a walk into the country around Cambridge during the Whitsun weekend. We were both in high spirits, and felt closer than ever. Half way to our destination, we sat down together to discuss our feeling for one another. In her subsequent comment on this discussion she recorded: "On Whitsunday, when we sat talking on the grass, I told you that you were the finest person I've ever met. I did mean it and I mean it still.

You are a real gentleman... and have a noble mind". I responded that I hoped that we would make our life together; and that I would be ready to wait until she reached the same conviction: however long that wait might be.

That was probably the last time we were together before Berit returned to Sweden to resume her acquaintance with her beloved horses as an assistant to the organisers of the Olympics, and to discuss options for a career in social work (she had already decided that an office occupation was not for her). The question on both our minds at that point was whether I should aim to spend part of the summer holiday with Berit's family in Sweden.

In her first letter to me from Stockholm, Berit felt compelled to warn me: "I don't think that what I feel for you is pure and final love... there isn't the all eclipsing love" that would lead to a commitment to a life together. She could not pretend otherwise. Would it not be sensible, therefore, for me to defer a trip to Sweden in order to avoid the risk that I might be deeply disappointed in my quest for her hand?

My reply was: "You must know that I want, above all things, to come to you in Stockholm; but you must know also that I can be in no way changed... I cannot give you up... you must seriously consider whether it would hurt you if I came to Stockholm".

These were the first exchanges in a voluminous correspondence that stretched over more than a year, interrupted only by my visits to Sweden in summer 1956 and 1957, and by Berit's return to Cambridge in June 1957 to join me, and other friends, for Pembroke College's May Ball. Through this period, Berit continued to agonise about her uncertainty about the depth of her feelings for me; and about her worries that she would hurt me more by seeing me again than by our keeping apart.

Further exchanges led to a firm conclusion that we both very much wanted me to come to Stockholm; and that I would be very welcome to stay at Berit's family's flat in Bromma. I therefore quickly booked a passage to Copenhagen on the Russian steamer SS Molotov, with the intention of motorcycling on to Stockholm through southern Sweden, so as to get a better picture of the country before meeting Berit again. (I had acquired a 1939 BSA motorcycle shortly before the end of the Cambridge summer term, and passed the driving test early in the summer vacation). I asked Berit to try to find a job to keep me occupied whilst she was working in a hospital to gain the practical experience she needed to enter the university course for social work.

So the die was cast! On 20 July I boarded the Molotov, my cycle was mounted on the ship's foredeck; and I was on my way to Sweden.

My only previous experience of the country had been on the journey to Oslo the previous summer, when a college friend and I camped overnight on the shore of a lake near Boras. The lady who owned a summer cottage overlooking the lake brought down to us a tray of coffee and "buns ("bullar") to round off our modest evening meal: a gesture of hospitality which made a great impression on us both!

My route through Sweden this time took me from Copenhagen and Halsingborg north east through the mainly pastoral countryside, interspersed with pine forests, to the east of Lake Vattern (where I camped for one night) and on to Stockholm: a journey of close to 300 miles. I was somewhat saddle-sore by the time I was greeted by Berit at 57 Rorlaggarvagen in Bromma - but relieved that my first long journey by motorcycle had ended successfully.

For the next four weeks - till I boarded SS Molotov again for the return journey to England - Berit and I spent the summer evenings and weekends together, and earned our living during the weekdays (she on a hospital ward; I weeding gladioli beds at a nursery where I had been taken on as an assistant gardener). It was an intoxicating experience to explore together the delights of Stockholm: to visit the royal palaces at Drottningholm and Gripsholm; to take the old-fashioned boats out to several of the islands that litter the Stockholm archipelago; to listen to concerts at the elegant modern town hall (Stadshuset) and view sculpture and paintings at a number of galleries; to enjoy excursions with Berit's parents to small towns outside Stockholm; to watch open air performances of plays in parks; but, above all, to rejoice in each other's arms at all the Swedish summer could offer. Not yet sure what the future might hold for us and our relationship, we were determined to make the most of what the present had to offer.

Berit's parents made me most welcome in the family flat. Since Berit's two elder brothers had left home, there was a spare bedroom for me; and Berit's mother, Margit, was adept and hospitable in preparing simple but attractive meals. Though they must have had some doubts about the strength and depth of our relationship - and whether a British son-in-law was a good thing - her parents put no obstacles in our way. I sensed that Berit was very close to her mother, but had little affection for her father, Georg. She judged him to be selfish, domineering and mean-spirited. That meant that there were occasions when there was some friction in interactions with him. But to me Georg was consistently cordial, if sometimes uncomfortably formal (for example, he expected me to address him in the third person: "would Uncle like to join us for a trip into town?").

All too soon, our time together drew to a close. I had booked a return passage on SS Molotov for 21 August; and Berit was committed to further assignments to give her practical experience of problems that a qualified social work professional must be able to cope with. We had not resolved the uncertainties and doubts about our futures. Berit continued to say : "Alan, my feelings for you are strong - but not strong enough to be real love. I think I'm still too young in many respects. I can't say anything definite now for the future." My response was typically on the lines of a letter written in August: "I think you know how happy I was to find you once again the Berit I thought I had lost. It will give me the greatest pleasure to have you to live for... and to share everything with. I love you with my heart, with my mind and with my body, with a completeness which I believe must come only once in a lifetime."

As we said our goodbyes on the pier where the Molotov was waiting, we agreed that we would keep in close touch through the resumption of our correspondence. My return to England was saved from moping by the company of several young Communists who were keen to discuss the differences we had about political means and ends. I was surprised and pleased that the discussion proceeded without animosity or posturing, with an acknowledgement on both sides of some of the weaknesses of the capitalist economy and Britain's liberal tradition, but serious questions whether the Communist Party's path to a classless society was sufficiently in touch with the aspirations of working people. (The invasion of Hungary by the Russian army had yet to happen; and its devastating impact on the confidence of western communists would only become evident towards the end of the year).

During the voyage home I composed a few stanzas of verse, dedicated to Berit, to convey something of the emotions I felt on leaving her behind in Sweden. Part of the poem reads:

"My hand cannot now touch yours. You may not now come near; And yet my voice may reach you And you perhaps still hear Me speak things dear to me."

"In the last fitful hour of sleeping before daybreak When past and future draw closer, Present is merged in prospect And reason not yet astir,
You stood at the threshold for me"

"Waiting. I reached in my bed for you But the sun forestalled us. Tomorrow shall I wait for you again?"

I returned to Cambridge that autumn invigorated by my experience of Stockholm, one of the most attractive, stylish and satisfying cities in Europe. I was excited by the prospect of renewing my correspondence with Berit; of pursuing the possibility of post-graduate study in America; and gearing up psychologically for my final year's work towards the Tripos Part II - and a degree.

Our letters to one another, over the period from October 1956 to midsummer 1957, (which numbered around 100!) covered a wide range of topics in which we were both keenly interested. For example, Berit's perceptive critique of the British for their hypocrisy and insularity: we are too polite to say what we really think; and too tied to our (declining!) empire to see that we have to give priority to developing our links with Europe and defending European civilisation. By contrast,I offered my reflections on the life of Albert Schweitzer, and my admiration for his philosophy that "The future of society depends on its worth to its individual members and not on the power of the state over the individual." We exchanged views about the situation of Hungary and Hungarians following the Russian invasion; and I confessed that my initial thought to travel to Vienna and offer my services to the organisation assisting the refugees was countered by the advice of the Austrian Embassy that my time would be better spent in Cambridge organising a lorry-load of emergency supplies to be sent to Vienna!

We discussed on many occasions our respective plans and aspirations for the future: plans which , for Berit, involved studying for a degree in social work in Stockholm; and for me graduate study in America and , after that, perhaps employment on the personnel side of industry or in the civil or foreign service. It seemed likely that the realisation of these objectives would involve lengthy separation: could we tolerate that?

We also commented on the decision of our mutual friends, Humphrey and Lionella to get married immediately after Humphrey's graduation.

They had come together during the early months of 1957, when Lionella had felt lost and lonely; and had fallen in love very quickly. Could two such different people make it together? Perhaps their differences (Lionella's need for love and reassurance would react positively with Humphrey's need to be admired) would help to build a solid relationship? We hoped!

As we moved into 1957, and nearer and nearer to my graduation (and a move to the United States), we returned often to the question: should we meet again, and on what understanding about our feelings for one another? I hoped that Berit would accept my invitation to be my guest at the Pembroke College May Ball; and join a party of several of the friends she had known during her time in Cambridge. This would be the social highlight of the year for me and for many of those graduating just before the date of the Ball. It would be an appropriate and enjoyable way of bidding farewell to our undergraduate days: the more so if Berit would join me for this last "Hurrah"!

I told Berit, in a letter written in March 1957, that "I shall be bitterly disappointed if you deny me the pleasure of going with you to the May Ball." After some hesitation, Berit could not resist the attraction of returning, however briefly, to the Cambridge she had loved, although confessing that "I am a little afraid of it all... afraid of meeting you again". So, on 15 June I was at Heathrow at 2 am to meet Berit off her flight from Stockholm; and we embarked on what I can only describe as an eight day "fiesta".

There was of course the Ball itself with a party of several of Berit's good friends and her cousin Synne, dancing to the music of Tommy Kinsman - and breakfasting, when the music died away, at a pub outside Cambridge. There was punting up the river to tea at Grantchester; and an open air performance of Midsummer Night's Dream in the gardens of (I think) Clare College. We celebrated Evensong at King's College, where Berit had so much enjoyed the Festival of Carols on Christmas Eve 1955. And we spent an evening in London, dining at El

Cubano, where espresso coffee was delivered through the spluttering Gaggia coffee machines then being introduced in London.

When she wrote an effusive letter of thanks the day after her return to Stockholm, she added: "The family ask whether you will be coming to Stockholm before you depart for America. What shall I tell them? Yes, I do want you to come. No doubt I'll be happy to have you here again. But still I'm hesitant... Oh this uncertainty - it's like poison." I needed no second invitation!

There was much to do before I could make the trip back to Sweden. A holiday with my family in Cornwall had been booked; and I did not feel I could cancel what might well be our last holiday together. Besides that, there were preparations for my journey to America where I was to take up the offer of a place at Cornell University. I eventually flew to Sweden in early August; and we then had no more than a week together before my return flight to London.

I cannot recall in any detail how we spent those precious few days. We were both uncomfortably aware how short a time we had together before we would have to separate again: possibly for a long time. We both recognised that we needed to reach some conclusion about our future relationship before we went our separate ways. What I recall most clearly was the intense closeness we felt on our final evening together; and the impact on us of our poring over the catalogue of the "Family of Man" Exhibition. This exhibition had been mounted and promoted by Edward Steichen; and Berit had seen it earlier that year when it appeared in Stockholm. She had been enormously impressed both by the quality of the photography and the emotional power of the images. As we leafed through the pages, we found ourselves responding to the range of human emotions displayed; and seeing in them some reflection of our own feelings. We seemed to become closer and closer, and any doubts we harboured about our commitment to one another dissolved. It was an extraordinary and overwhelming experience for us both.

When Berit next wrote to me - on 11 August - there was a new confidence and certainty that had not been evident before: "My darling Alan. I'm falling in love with you... it is so much stronger than it looks on paper. It means that I want to marry you, that I want to raise a family with you, that I want to share life, difficulties and pleasure, all its beauties, with you..."

It was enough to send me on my way rejoicing.

CROSSING THE ATLANTIC

After returning from Stockholm, via Copenhagen, I had little more than a week to prepare for my journey to New York and beyond. There was much to be done: shopping for suitable clothes for a colder climate; making sure that my documentation would satisfy the American immigration officers; informing friends about my imminent departure; and , of course, keeping in good touch with Berit. What I did not - could not - find time for was to let my mother and Aunt Barbara know of Berit's and my decision to get married as soon as we had both completed our respective university courses.

I was cautious about speaking to my mother about my strong feelings for Berit. I recalled how upset I had been about my mother's response to my short-lived relationship with Ann(" You cannot be serious about marrying a baker's daughter" had been her comment!). I was unwilling to court a similarly negative reaction to Berit. I judged that there would not be time for lengthy discussion of our plans; and I was afraid that such a discussion would have been emotionally charged and leave us saying things we would later regret. I persuaded myself that it would be best to write to my mother to explain things after I had settled in Ithaca.

That letter was written during the autumn. It elicited from my mother the most loving and positive response I had ever had from her. All she wanted was my happiness and success in my career. She understood and accepted my wish to marry Berit; and emphasized that Berit would be a welcome addition to the family. She slipped into the envelope containing her letter, without comment (!), a short poem that sufficiently explained how she felt about my plans.

It read as follows:

So I will let you go, my son I will let you go.
Though grief must tarry gently now, I can let you go.

Though laughter and your sudden smile, Your leaping up the stair
And all you loving kindliness To ease my care

Are gone with your swift striding feet To roads I shall not roam,
O think not mine to be a love That bade you stay at home."

I was deeply touched by mother's letter and the poem. But I was
also hurt: for it brought home to me the gap I had allowed to grow
between us over the past year or more, and the pain that must have
caused. However, I felt that I could look forward to a less fraught
and closer relationship in the future. My tears were of joy rather than
regret and rancour!

*****

Despite my misgivings and disappointment about the probable
lengthy separation from Berit whilst we pursued our courses in
different countries, I boarded the TSS New York - a Greek-owned
liner, built in Britain and crewed by Germans - at Southampton
on 20 August with a keen excitement about what lay ahead. The
passengers were predominantly young American female college
students returning home after touring the major European cities. We
had many opportunities during the voyage to New York to exchange
views about their experience of Europe; and I to gain some insights
about America.

In my notes about the voyage, I observed the "youthful vitality and
zest for life" of the young women I spoke to; and their confidence ,
emphasised by their education, in the "American way". I also noted
how important it was to these college students to take part in , to
join and make a show in community activities of all kinds. They felt
confident about their position of equality with their male peers: in

any partnership they would expect to hold their own! I noted, too, a marked tendency of these students to wish to become linked with a settled and committed male partner: often to the extent of having a firm relationship from their High School days. This tendency was perhaps accentuated by what is called pinning - that is the exchange of Fraternity pins, a recognised preliminary to formal engagement. I could not help wondering whether the urge to early marriage (and family formation) might not restrict in important ways their future career choices and make them less able in the long run to maintain the gender equality they claimed. (The word "feminism" was on nobody's lips ! It would be for their children's generation to campaign for the Equal Rights Amendment to the US Constitution)

*****

We arrived in New York in dismal weather, with the Statue of Liberty shrouded in mist; and the outline of the skyscrapers barely visible. After mooring, we waited five hours to clear customs and immigration formalities! But Tom Metcalf, a friend with whom I had travelled to the Pyrenees in the spring, was there to meet me. He whisked me down the New Jersey Turnpike (Motorway) to spend several days as guest of his family at their home ten miles from Philadelphia. I was made very welcome; and taken on a tour of Philadelphia to make my obeisance at that shrine of American independence: Independence Hall, where the Declaration of Independence was signed in 1776; and the American Constitution was debated and signed in 1787.

What I enjoyed as much as anything during my stay with the Metcalfs was the trip Tom and I took into the Appalachian Mountains. We climbed up a part of the long trail which had been cut into these mountains from the State of Maine in the north to Georgia in the Deep South. We looked down into the Delaware Water Gap over the countryside which was the scene of several of the battles in the War of Independence.

An appropriate place to begin my American Odyssey!

From Philadelphia the Metcalfs drove me north to Boston to stay with Lennie Wharton and his family in Brookline, a city just outside Boston. Lennie was the other American friend with whom I travelled to the Pyrenees; and we had become very good friends during my last year in Cambridge. Lennie's close-knit family was Jewish - and devotedly so. I was made welcome to their celebration of traditional Jewish family ceremonies, including the formal engagement of Lennie to his longtime sweetheart, Judy. Judy and Lennie conducted me on a tour of Boston (again, a suitable bow to the crucial role that Boston had played in the founding of USA). We ended up the tour, across the Charles River, at Harvard Yard, the central focal point of Harvard University. There the ivy-covered red brick buildings carried a hint of the powerful ambition of the University to be at least the equal of the Cambridge from which I had graduated. I was not ashamed to underline the fact that Harvard had been founded during the time my ancestor, John Winthrop , had been Governor of Massachusetts; and that its foundation was assisted by the generosity of John Harvard, who had been a graduate of Cambridge University. I could feel some pride, therefore, in the British heritage of Harvard.

However, I was not there to claim a place at Harvard. It was time to move on to Cornell. The journey from Boston to Ithaca - a distance of some 300 miles - was by Greyhound Bus, the widely used nation- wide service for journeys to places ill-served by railroads. It took thirteen hours, with intervening stops at several cities to take on more passengers and to provide refreshment facilities for hungry and thirsty travellers. I was very weary by the time we reached Ithaca, and I climbed the steep hill which led up to the Cornell University campus.

*****

I had arrived in Ithaca early in September, some ten days before the start of the academic year - and before my room in the graduate residential quarters was ready for occupation. I therefore had the opportunity to explore the campus; discover something about my new "Alma mater"; and do some preliminary reading in readiness for the start of the semester.

I had been told that Cornell had the reputation of being the most beautiful campus in the country. I could see why. It was perched on a hill high above the town of Ithaca, with an impressive view over Lake Cayuga and the Finger Lakes region to the north, and tree clad hills to the west. Immediately below the main campus were two creeks and a lake; and the campus embraced its own golf course, and superb botanical gardens. The accommodation was an eclectic mixture of styles, without the cloistered quadrangles that, in Cambridge Colleges, help to create a sense of community. The sporting facilities were generous and would surely serve to stimulate a powerful loyalty to The Big Red football squad.

I soon learned that Cornell was founded in 1865 by Ezra Cornell (its first benefactor) and Andrew Dickson White (its first President, who insisted that the University should be able to teach any student any subject!). The University was the youngest of the Ivy League colleges (a group of prestigious private institutions, mainly founded in the colonial period, who formed an athletic association to oversee competitions in a range of sports between its eight participating members). In one respect, Cornell was a pioneer: from its beginning it was a co-educational college, welcoming suitably qualified girls as well as boys. It was also different from other Ivy League colleges in being a so-called Land Grant institution, enjoying financial support from the State Legislature of New York. Moreover, in the course of time four statutory colleges - offshoots of the State University - were established on the Cornell campus, and became part of the University.

One of these State University bodies was the New York State School of Industrial and Labor Relations(NYSSILR), to which I was heading.

On first acquaintance, the ILR (as I shall call it) was an incongruous neighbour to other university departments. It consisted of a number of Quonset (in Britain "Nissen") hutments which appeared out of character with the rest of Cornell. These huts created the impression of being pioneers of a not-yet-firmly established discipline. In many respects this impression was correct. The ILR had been founded in 1945 by the State legislature, at a time when there was a bitter debate about the laws governing industrial relations. The objective was to bring into debates a better understanding of factors influencing the behaviour of people in the workplace, and to offer to both sides of industry a resource (Outreach) to assist in the resolution of disputes. During the period from 1945 to the middle fifties the ILR had gained a solid reputation for sound academic scholarship combined with excellent contacts with industry and an impartial approach to the legal and political issues that bedevilled industrial relations. Several of the senior professors who had been founder members of the ILR were still in post when I arrived at Ithaca; and I was deeply impressed both by their wisdom and skills as teachers and by the way that they set the standard for the younger up-and-coming professors.

In the week before term started - when I could find few professors to guide me - I settled down in the well stocked ILR library to study a book that I dimly recalled to have been one of the earliest and most influential works on human relations in the workplace. It bore the simple title: Management and the Worker; and it s authors were two Harvard academics: Roethlisberger and Dickson. Published in 1939, it detailed the course and results of ground-breaking experiments conducted within the Hawthorne plant of the Western Electric company. These experiments were designed to measure the impact on productivity of a variety of changes to working practices, hours of work, pauses in work for refreshment etc. The researchers found that almost all the changes had a positive impact on output and morale. Moreover, the more frequent the interactions of managers and supervisors with the two groups of workers at the centre of the experiments, the more positive the responses of the workers.

These results - obvious and almost banal as they may now appear - had a widespread and significant influence on many companies' approach to problems of motivation and morale - and gave rise to what came to be called "the Hawthorne effect". This study proved to be an excellent preparation for the courses in human relations I subsequently took; and opened my eyes to new research methods for engaging with human problems in the workplace (with benefits to the research I would myself undertake).

*****

By the end of September, I had moved into my room at the hall of residence established for graduate students: Cascadilla Hall. It was a rather dismal three-storey building, with few frills (no catering facilities, and not even a room for social activities and coffee!). But my room was reasonably ample, and a good breakfast could be had at a small cafe across the road for 50 cents.

More significantly, I had met up with the professors who were to be my supervisors; and had agreed the main thrust of course work I would undertake. I decided, at the outset, that my main objective during my time at the ILR school would be to achieve the degree of Master of Science (MS). This would involve a focus on two major topics: Human Relations in Industry; and the history and practice of collective bargaining(and the legal framework within which collective bargaining was ordered). The MS degree also entailed the writing of a thesis involving some basic research and field work. I could already see that I had more than a year's hard graft to achieve the degree; and that I should almost certainly need to forego any summer holiday break to concentrate on the work for my thesis!

I had been warned, soon after I arrived at Cornell, that, even at graduate level, there was a large degree of prescription about required reading and topics for study: quite different from what a

European graduate student would expect. I must also adjust to the frequency of tests and exams that punctuated the curriculum. Woe betide the student who decided what books s/he would read, rather than follow the prescribed texts. To a certain extent, this pattern of learning constrained initiative; but after a while I was able to adapt to this regime. In this I had two advantages: I had more experience in writing essays against time pressures than was typical among American students. More important, the professor who was my main supervisor, Henry Landsberger, had fled the Nazi regime as a boy, and had been educated mainly in England. He understood European culture, and was notably sympathetic in helping me to adjust to American norms. He was also a formidable scholar and made himself easily available to me if I had any problems to discuss. We became very good friends over the following 18 months; and maintained that friendship long after I had left Ithaca.

One happy result of my adaptation to the learning regime was that I scored high enough marks - and presumably earned enough credit with my professors - to be awarded a Graduate Assistantship in January 1958. This not only offered a "salary" of $180/month but reduced the level of fees for the course at ILR by 50% - in exchange for a modicum of support for one of the more senior professors in eg marking undergraduate papers or leading seminars for undergraduate courses. This greatly eased the financial pressures on me. It also enabled me to buy a second hand Dodge (at $225), and considerably widened my opportunities for travel.

*****

One of the pleasures and advantages of my time at Cornell was the opportunity to develop friendships with a number of (mainly) overseas students who were studying the same subjects as I was. Very early on, I met up with Sandip Sen and Jane Billing. Sandip had been brought up in a Calcutta family with a strong admiration for the British Raj. He spoke and wrote stylish English; and had a delightfully Anglo/Indian sense of humour. He would regale us with anecdotes about the way Indian families selected marriage partners for their offspring. He also had a fund of stories about the chancy character of working in an Indian company. Jane was an Oxford graduate who had fallen in love with an American Congregationalist minister, whom she expected to marry on leaving Cornell . She had a low key personality, but opened up readily to reveal a wry sense of humour - and many perceptive observations about American culture (often unfavourable!).

We three were soon joined by Lilian Holmsen, who had fled from Russian controlled Estonia as a girl; and had been educated in Sweden. An enterprising young woman,she had migrated from Sweden to Canada - and there married a Norwegian, Andreas. They had planned to develop their respective careers in the USA. Lilian frequently commented on the narrowness of the American approach to education. Then there was Renda Spiele, a Dutch lawyer with substantial experience in personnel work in Holland. She was forthright, ebullient and very sociable: she was sure to make a first class Personnel Director when she returned home. Another character was Hiroko Yokota, a Japanese lady who had struggled to achieve any advance in her career at home. She had come to Cornell to improve her prospects. She was our first "feminist": determined to enhance the status and opportunities of Japanese women in a male- dominated culture. We were soon joined by two American women: Pat Hammond and Ruth Dubin. Pat came from North Carolina with an idealist's determination to support efforts to unionise textile firms in that state. Ruth was a clear-headed realist, well schooled in psychology, who had an acute understanding of the springs of enmity in the industrial relations world.

We would sometimes gather at Lilian's digs for a pre-exam discussion of the issues we expected to confront the next day: wine and coffee eased the thought process. More often several of us had informal gatherings over lunch or an evening meal to compare notes on our progress - or lack of it. We all felt we gained much from the differing experiences we brought to discussions of the American scene. I am left with two reflections about this group: first, its very existence illustrates the generosity of New York State in enabling so many overseas graduates to sample American opportunities. Secondly, it is perhaps surprising that no American male joined the group: perhaps a reflection of the fact that the most capable male graduates with a keen interest in industrial relations preferred to head for law school, where labor law was an important, expanding and rewarding speciality?

*****

Through the long winter months, when the Cornell campus was under snow for much of the period from January to March, Berit and I pursued various options to enable us to spend the summer together in Ithaca. We eventually decided that the most practical course would be for Berit to seek a job as a family help/au pair, hopefully allowing her sufficient free time to compose a thesis (on the role of the International Labour Organisation) which her supervisors at Stockholm's Social Institute had agreed to accept as a suitable alternative to a summer work placement.

This plan worked out much as we hoped. I advertised in the Ithaca press for a family wishing to engage a temporary help over the summer months; and we found a couple with Finnish ancestors who liked the idea of engaging someone from northern Europe. A deal was done - and the US Immigration authorities made no demur, provided they received a formal signed Affidavit from the host family guaranteeing that Berit would be employed and accommodated without cost to the American taxpayer.

Thus it was that, in mid June, I met Berit off the plane at Idlewild (Now Kennedy) airport; and we travelled back to Ithaca in Pandora (the name we had given our car). I had joined with Sandip to rent an apartment overlooking Cascadilla Gorge for the summer whilst Berit lived with the Soyring family as a family help.

In the absence of correspondence during this marvellous break, I cannot recall in any detail how we exploited this time together. We saw a good deal of the Holmsens and Sandip; and of Henry and Betty Landsberger. Berit scoured the ILR library for material on the history and role of the ILO; and must have worked diligently on her thesis. She also gave me much help in organising the material I was gathering for my thesis. We managed to fit in a trip to Niagara Falls, about 100 miles distant from Ithaca. We also visited Washington and New York; and spent an idyllic and relaxing week with the Holmsens at a lakeside retreat north of Ottawa in Canada. For the most part, though, we used our free hours walking and talking together, reviving the love we could not completely express in letters. It was rather like a pre-Honeymoon!

*****

From the time Berit returned to Sweden in September to the conclusion of my stay in Ithaca, I was largely preoccupied with two challenges: the first was to complete my thesis in time to depart for home at the end of February 1959. The second was to make some progress in planning a future beyond Cornell.

The topic I had chosen for my thesis, with encouragement and advice from Henry Landsberger, was "the sense of responsibility among young workers": that is, very broadly, to assess the factors which combine to make young workers more responsible in carrying out their tasks in the workplace. The study was based on supermarket employees (between the ages of 18 and 25) in stores of the Loblaw Inc supermarket chain in northeast USA.

The study faced several challenges: to define satisfactorily what is "a sense of responsibility", distinguishing this from a range of other characteristics which may typify the "good worker"; to measure the extent to which young workers possess that quality; and to relate "responsibility scores" to variables in the individual which might explain (in technical terms to correlate with) such scores. What made these challenges more difficult was the fact that my population of (99) young workers was relatively small and spread over 18 stores; and it was difficult to be sure that standards of judgement by managers in each of these stores were reasonably consistent.

I was fortunate to have the support of all levels of management in Loblaw, who saw potential personnel and commercial advantages in the study. I was even more fortunate that only one of my sample of 99 workers failed to complete the questionnaires I asked of them.

Nonetheless, as the questionnaires were returned to me in late September, I became increasingly aware of the problems of deriving credible , and statistically valid, inferences from the material; and of the shortage of time to write up the study by my deadline. Towards the end of January 1959, I was still frantically working all hours to get a final draft into the hands of the secretary who had agreed to type my manuscript into a document that I could present to my examiners. It just worked! And Henry Landsberger and the other examining professors found it possible to accept the thesis (now in a handsome bound volume) as a satisfactory contribution to my overall work for a Master of Science degree. (A summary report of my investigation was published in the journal of Occupational Psychology in 1960. Although I was described as the "senior author", much of the drafting was the work of Henry Landsberger, since I had by January 1960 departed the ILR school)

I was delighted (and relieved) to clear this hurdle and claim my MS degree. I was even more delighted to receive from the Cornell authorities a formal notice that I had been elected to membership of the Phi Kappa Phi Fraternity in recognition that my course and exam marks of over 90% placed me in the top 5% of graduate students at the University. This was a satisfying end result of an enjoyable and rewarding 18 months' effort.

*****

At the time I landed at ILR, I had no firm or clear plans for what I might do after completing the course at Cornell. I had made only a few desultory approaches to possible future employers, since I would be out of Britain for a year or more, and not available for interviews etc. My intention in transferring from Cambridge to Cornell was to make myself better prepared for the world of work beyond University (and better placed to decide what would be the most attractive field of work).

The content of the ILR course might suggest that employment in the personnel division of an international firm would be an appropriate objective for me; and this was certainly a possibility that was in my mind up to the end of 1958. But the more I pondered this option, the more I was attracted by the alternative possibility of a career in the British Civil Service (and in particular in a department with a focus on industrial enterprise and labour relations). This was prompted in part by the thought that Government service might offer wider opportunities to influence policy in fields where British companies were often notably backward .

I therefore decided to enter the Civil Service competition for entry to (what was then known as) the Administrative Class, which offered a route to the most senior policy posts advising Ministers. This competition involved three stages, at each of which weaker candidates were weeded out: an initial written test; then a series of practical tests and interviews over a three-day period; and ,finally, an interview by the Final Selection Board (FSB) chaired by the Civil Service Commissioner. I was in no doubt that this was a highly competitive situation; but I comforted myself with the reflection that failure would not be not the end of the world!

I sat the first stage of the competition while I was briefly home in England over Christmas 1958. My mother cabled me, after I returned to Ithaca in January, to let me know that I had passed the written test; and that I could expect to be called to attend the second stage in London some time in March. In the event, I was able to fit in this commitment before I departed to Stockholm for my marriage to Berit at Easter 1959. I was then on tenterhooks for several weeks, whilst on honeymoon in southern Sweden: waiting to hear whether I would be called to the Final Selection Board, and, if so, whether the date would interfere with our honeymoon.

My luck held! Yes: I was to attend the FSB; and NO: the date would not require any adjustment to our honeymoon trip. I flew back to London for the FSB in late April; and heard, a few days later, that I had cleared this final hurdle - and, wonder of wonders ,was to be posted to the Ministry of Labour, my first choice.

This outcome was , I judged, a highly satisfying start to a new career: as husband and provider. To this career I turn in the second part of this Memoir.

James Brown (my father)

Mummy and Alan,
May 1934

My English nanny and
Alan, March 1934

A nanny and Alan, Gold
Coast at 8 and half months

Alan and his Aunt (Barabara
Winthrop), Accra 1936

Shirley and Alan with a
nanny in Achimota 1936

Jenny Watkins, Shirley and Alan at
beach hut on Gold Coast

Alan with Scruffy, 1938

Shirley and Alan
(and Celeste)
April 1940, Cape Town

St Georges Cathedral
School, Cape Town

Swimming pool my father designed
and built at Achimoto

Fun on the beach at Accra with my
father November 1941

Mummy, Achimota

Achimota College
Admin Block

First day of boarding school
Cape Town August 1941

Alan, Claremont,
South Africa 1943

Shirley and Alan,
Cape Town 1943

Alan and Jenny,
Melton Wold, South Af rica in 1942

Bedford School

Pembroke College, Cambridge,
New Court

Pembroke College Library, Cambridge

Pembroke College, Cambridge

Cornell University

Cornell University

PART TWO: A PARTNERSHIP

WEDDING BELLS

Berit and I announced our engagement on Christmas Eve 1958.

She had flown from Sweden a few days earlier to spend the Christmas break with my family in Pirbright; whilst I had flown from New York with similar intent. I had also planned to take the first part of the competition for the civil service administrative grade in early January.

We seized the opportunity to get away together for a day in Cambridge, which had such happy memories for both of us. In a quiet side street off Trumpington Street I slipped a diamond ring on Berit's finger; and kissed her good luck. We then proceeded to King's College Chapel to hear the traditional service of lessons and carols, which had so moved Berit when she first came to Cambridge three years earlier.

There can be few more sublime experiences than hearing, in the semi darkness, the first verse of " Once in Royal David's City" sung by a young chorister as the choir progresses from the west door down the long nave to their seats at the east end. The unbroken male voice has such purity and clarity to move anyone to tears. The service that followed provided a joyful celebration of our "official" engagement - and the most appropriate prelude to the days we were to share with my family over Christmas.(we retain to this day a recording of this service, conducted by David Willcocks; and we often replay it on Christmas Eve).

We had long planned to get married at Easter 1959 in Bromma Church, the oldest church in Sweden to have been in continuous use as a place of worship. But there were important hurdles to clear before that plan could be realized: not the least of these was to satisfy the Swedish church authorities that I was suitably qualified to allow the Banns of Marriage to be published. Happily, I was able to return to England with my MS degree from Cornell University in time to complete preparations for the wedding , and to travel to Stockholm several days before "Lysningsdag" (this is the day the Banns are announced). This is traditionally the occasion when relatives and close friends descend on the prospective Bride's home to deliver their wedding presents - and enjoy a generous supply of coffee and cakes, with much discussion about the couple's plans for the future. (I have often wondered why this practice has not been introduced in Britain!).

In the run up to the wedding, my family (my mother and Aunt Barbara, together with Joyce and Charles Lyle who had been such loyal and generous friends over so many years that I counted them as "family") arrived in Stockholm to celebrate the wedding. They had time for some exploration of Stockholm; and were entertained by Margit and Georg Ohlson, Berit's parents, to a performance of Hugo Alfven's ballet "Swedish Rhapsody" at the Stockholm Opera . They were also taken by Georg to see the South Hospital (Sodersjhukhuset) where Georg was Superintendent (Chief Executive). This was the most modern, and also the largest, hospital in Europe; and my family were suitably impressed by this evidence of the quality of health care in Sweden. (Clearly, Georg was a very significant figure in delivering health services!)

Easter Saturday dawned grey and chill, with little sign of early spring. But it was , happily, dry. After Berit and I had dressed suitably for the occasion (Berit with a delightful "crown" of lilies of the valley; I with a white rose in my buttonhole), we progressed to Bromma Church, where a gathering of thirty or more (mainly family) waited. Bengt Kolste, the senior parish priest, conducted the wedding service, in Swedish. My halting command of the language made it difficult to grasp some of the detail of the proceedings. But I did understand that Rev Kolste, mindful that Berit's first name was Rut ,reminded us of the story of the Biblical Ruth who left her country to settle and marry, happily,far from her natal home. He wished us similar happiness. But he was not aware that Berit heartily disliked her first name, and would not have wished to draw attention to it! (moreover, he would not have known that the best remembered reference to Ruth in English was in Keats' poem "Ode to a Nightingale", where the poet writes of "the sad heart of Ruth when, sick for home, She stood in tears amid the alien corn").

I doubt whether anyone in the congregation worried much about these objections: certainly Berit and I were too excited to pay much attention to the fortunes of Ruth!

After the wedding service, and still with fragments of confetti in our hair, we repaired for the wedding feast to Stallmastaregarden (an ancient hostelry much patronised by newly married couples) to which Margit and Georg had invited about 20 guests (including my family of four) to celebrate our marriage. Georg made a courteous short speech in English to welcome the members of my family and to say how happy he and Margit were to have me in theirs. To my shame, I did not - could not- -respond in Swedish to express our gratitude to Georg and Margit for making us all so welcome and providing so generous a feast!

Soon afterwards Berit and I said our farewells to the guests and set off to change for the flight to Halmstad on the first stage of our honeymoon in southern Sweden. And it was in Halmstad that we spent our first night as man and wife.

After a suitably lavish breakfast the following morning, we met up with Berit's aunt, Siv, who had generously offered us, as a wedding gift, the loan of a car to enable us to explore at leisure the southern counties of Sweden.

I cannot recall much of our travels over the following ten days. Certainly we spent several days in a charming "pension" in Molle at the northern tip of Skane, overlooking the straits of Oresund with a distant view of Denmark. After that, we must have visited Lund and its cathedral, designed in the style of a Roman basilica, with a prominent Romanesque apse to offset the solidity of the building. After Lund, we explored several towns in Blekinge and Smaland; and I remember being impressed with Glimmingehus, one of the oldest secular buildings , and the best preserved medieval fortress, in southern Sweden. Not far from there was the centre of fine glassmaking in Kosta, Boda and Orrefors; and we spent a day going round factories in this area, marvelling at the skills of the glassblowers and the superb quality of their products .

On our way back to return our Volvo, we stopped off at Almhult, where IKEA had recently established their main workshop and design/administrative centre and its first retail shop - and would soon become famous throughout Sweden, and beyond, for their flatpack and competitively-priced furniture.

On our return to Stockholm it was time to get to work. Berit had a further work placement to complete over the summer months before she could become a qualified social worker. I found, through Georg's connections, a job as under-gardener at Beckomberga Hospital, a large psychiatric institution on the outskirts of Stockholm. I worked , with about six others, under the benign and relaxed supervision of "Tradgardsmastare" (head gardener) Liljestam, on the maintenance of the hospital's substantial estate . It was not a demanding job; there were several coffee breaks during the day; and the month of May was interrupted by three public holidays followed by the Midsummer celebrations in June.

After a brief period when we shared a flat with Berit's brother Jan and his wife, Ulrika, we rented a flat in the centre of Stockholm (notionally shared with another couple who were almost never in residence) at a very reasonable rental cost. The flat was ideally located for weekend trips into the Stockholm archipelago (Skargarden) as well as other attractions of the city and the surrounding area. We were blessed with almost unbroken fine and sunny weather throughout the summer months, which made our weekend breaks a delight. I look back on the six months we spent together in Stockholm as an extended honeymoon!

However, towards the end of September it was time for me to say goodbye to Stockholm, and to begin preparations for setting up home in England.

For all the attractions of Sweden, we had always expected - perhaps selfishly on my part - that we would make our home in this country. My halting Swedish, though just about adequate for day-to-day purposes, would have severely limited my prospects on the Swedish jobs market; whilst Berit's social work qualifications, combined with her fluency in English, would make her a highly desirable addition to Britain's work force. Moreover, I had already been appointed to a post in the British civil service which offered the prospect of an attractive career. Though we hoped to maintain very close and frequent contacts with Sweden, it was therefore to Britain we looked for establishing our permanent base.

My first task on returning to England (without Berit, whose course assignments would not be completed before November) was to find us a place to live. We were looking for a two-bedroom flat, within reasonable distance of London, affordable, with central heating and in a good state of repair. Moreover, my quest had to be achieved before I started work in the first week of October. Most of my mother's friends commented: "You'll be lucky"!

Three things were in our favour. From my modest investment in Treasury gilts, I reckoned I could put down a deposit of around £750. There was a late 1950s spate of new building and an active housing market. And interest rates were low (about 2½ %, as I recall).

In a hectic week, I scoured the newspapers for properties on the outskirts of London; and visited a handful of "possibles". In the end, it seemed to me to boil down to a choice between a late Victorian flat in Putney and a newly built flat, with underfloor heating, just off the Great West Road(and just off the flightpath of planes approaching Heathrow Airport). I telegraphed this news to Berit, with a recommendation in favour of the newly built option, at a price of £2750. Berit signalled her agreement; and before the week was out I had cut a deal on Sefton Court: a flat on the third storey of a development of around 50 flats. Within little more than a week, we had committed to a new home that, we hoped, would be ready for occupation in November.

The family solicitor, to whom I turned for the conveyancing work, was of the old school: he clearly wondered if I knew what I was letting myself in for. Did I realise, for example, that I would have to pay annual maintenance charges to the property manager, which the 99 year lease gave me no opportunity to challenge? I was naive enough to hope that a new development would not need much maintenance in its early years! I signed the contract: and soon had arranged a mortgage for £2000 to complete the purchase.

Yes, we were lucky!

It was now time to devote myself to Her Majesty's business.

A NEW START

I started work at the Ministry of Labour and National Service (as it was then called) as an Assistant Principal in the Health and Safety Division on 5 October 1959. I was one of a dozen APs, of varying seniority, filling training posts for senior positions in the Department: all of us based at offices in and around St James's Square, half a mile from the Government heartland of Whitehall.

I had been living, studying or working outside Britain for virtually all of the previous two years before throwing in my lot with the civil service. I wondered how much had changed since I left Cambridge.

A first impression was how relatively calm and settled the country seemed. This impression appeared to be confirmed by the outcome of the General Election held on 8 October: the governing Party, the Conservatives, won nearly 50% of the vote, and secured an overall majority in the House of Commons of 100 seats. When I left for the United States in August 1957 the country was still recovering from the bitter political division resulting from the ill-fated Suez invasion of October 1956; and the humiliating withdrawal forced on the British and French forces by President Eisenhower. Since then, Harold Macmillan (who had taken over as Prime Minister from the ailing Anthony Eden) had presided over a recovery of morale of the government and a significant improvement in the economy. He had also begun to reconcile the country to the post-Suez reality of the country's declining power and influence in the world, and the thrust towards independence of significant parts of the British Empire.

A second impression was that the country seemed well off materially. There was, it struck me, a sense of optimism about the future standard of living. This was illustrated, for example, by the widespread ownership of television sets: indeed the 1959 election campaign was largely conducted through TV broadcasting channels. The reduction of ninepence in the pound on income tax reinforced an impression that the economy was progressing steadily in the right direction.

Thirdly, however, the general sense of wellbeing could not mask the racial tensions resulting from the substantial flows of Commonwealth immigrants from the Caribbean and the Indian sub-continent. The Notting Hill riots in August 1958 were only an extreme example of the underlying problems of integrating the immigrants into British society.

Fourthly, it was more and more evident that, whilst the Federal Republic of Germany was becoming a booming and prosperous powerhouse, Britain was an under-performing laggard, its growth rate and productivity falling far behind the rest of Western Europe. The Macmillan government had yet to address the implications of economic weakness; and only a minority of Ministers and senior officials had begun to wonder whether the country might benefit from a closer engagement with the EEC (Common Market). It was already clear, by the end of 1959, that the EEC was likely to become a major economic force; and that the country's future prosperity could not be sustained entirely through traditional trading links with the Commonwealth countries and the United States.

Some indication of these latter concerns (about economic growth and productivity) was evident in the early discussions I had with my colleagues - often round the lunch table in the Ministry's canteen - as I settled in to my official seat. Many senior officials appeared to feel that the Ministry of Labour had not sufficiently addressed some problems that seriously impeded the country's economic progress.

The first of these was the disorderly state of industrial relations in significant areas of British industry. To the general public this was brought home by the large number of unofficial strikes. But the problem was much wider than that: inadequate procedure agreements governing the calling of strikes; poor management; inter-union disputes about representation of workers in different trades; the lack of effective legal limitations on the actions of shop stewards calling strikes without the agreement of their trade unions: these were all important factors in many industrial disputes. Successive governments since the War had done little to regulate industrial disputes;, and there was now growing pressure for a bolder and more determined search for effective measures to introduce a more disciplined and responsible approach to relations between employers and trade unions.

A second area of concern was the inadequate provision of training opportunities, particularly for young entrants to the labour market. The dearth of apprenticeships of satisfactory quality was seen as a major constraint on economic growth and productivity; but many employers were unwilling to invest in training if the people they trained were likely to be "poached" by other employers.

Thirdly, there was little agreement among economists - or politicians! - about how to achieve a higher level of productivity and ensure that pay settlements took proper account of the ability of industry to absorb their cost without driving up inflation.

Fourth, there was much talk about the so-called "dole queue" image of the country's Employment Exchanges. Though they were efficient in paying unemployment benefit , Exchanges were seen as unattractive places for workers to go to look for work-- or for employers to use in filling their vacancies. This reduced the effectiveness of the public employment service in promoting an efficient labour market.

I looked forward to playing some part in developing policies to deal with these problems. In the meantime, my main immediate responsibility was to edit the Annual Report of the Chief Inspector of Factories, detailing, among other matters, the number of fatal and serious accidents to factory workers (which cost much more in lost output than industrial disputes!). Much of my first posting was therefore spent in getting to know how the Factory Inspectorate operated; and what they saw as the main risks to factory workers. I had frequent discussions with the Chief Inspector himself, which illuminated for me the way he led and managed his inspectors, and set their priorities. What struck me most forcibly was the intense sense of personal responsibility of the individual inspectors: both in deciding where to focus their scrutiny and how to respond to the many horrible accidents they had to investigate. They operated in a much more independent way than most other employees in the Ministry - and this had a marked effect on the culture of the organisation, and tended to distance the Inspectorate from the rest of the Ministry of Labour. My very modest contributions to reviewing the work of the Inspectorate culminated in the publication of the Annual Report in September 1960 - and a generous lunch with the Chief Inspector after he had presented his report to the Press. That marked the conclusion of my first post in the Department (it was the normal practice for Assistant Principals to be assigned to policy divisions for a period of around a year before being moved on to a new post).

******

Whilst I was getting my feet under the table in a rather cramped office, and beginning to acquire some of the habits and skills of a civil servant, Berit was completing her degree course at the Social Institute in Stockholm. By mid-November she had gained her qualification as a social worker; and was ready to set off for England to make her home in the flat we had bought on the western edge of London : 50 Sefton Court.

It was several weeks before we could take possession - and even when we did I recall that on our first night we had no electricity: we slept in a cold kitchen with heat supplied by the gas cooker; and there was no telephone! Over the following couple of months we acquired and installed the most necessary items of furniture, and made ourselves comfortable with the electric underfloor heating, which was a novel feature of this development(however it did not heat the kitchen or bathroom!). Berit became familiar with key features of the locality: shopping at Sainsbury's old fashioned grocery store; the train service on the Piccadilly Line of the London Underground; the local parks which provided some relief from the incessant traffic on the Great West Road; and the journey to Pirbright, where we spent several weekends and the Christmas holiday with my mother and Aunt at Bakersgate Cottage.

Berit did not begin to think about employment until the New Year (after she had served as Maid of Honour at the wedding of my sister Shirley and David Head in early January). She then began to make tentative enquiries about the prospect of employment in the Children's Department of London County Council. In next to no time she found herself offered a post as a children's officer with a team responsible for the welfare of children in an area around King's Cross. Though she was uneasy about being thrust into service so quickly, and in such a challenging district, she was reassured that her prospective boss regarded her qualification and experience as ideal for this work. She was also assured that a thorough training course would give her a good basic preparation for her responsibilities. She decided to take the plunge.

Berit was fortunate to join a team of mainly experienced social workers, who supported her (and each other) and made her very welcome. But the situation was very challenging, not to say stressful. The area around King's Cross had a very mixed population: in nationality, race, family situation, and length of time in the area. There were numerous families of Greek, Cypriot, West Indian and Irish extraction; and many children were in dysfunctional families, often with absentee or non-existent fathers. The attitude towards the intervention of social workers was often hostile or suspicious. Added to that, Berit had to commute from Hounslow to King's Cross: a daily journey of around forty five minutes in each direction. Altogether a much more taxing employment than mine!

I was amazed how well Berit coped with the strain. She was clearly greatly helped by the constructive rapport she struck up with her colleagues. But there was one important downside. We had decided ,early in the year, that we would like to start a family. As the months passed with no sign of pregnancy, Berit began to wonder whether the strains of the job were militating against her becoming pregnant. With some reluctance, she decided in November to hand in her notice to the Children's Department; and by Christmas she had given up her post. She received a glowing testimonial from the head of her area team: a tribute to her resilience and perhaps also to the thorough training she had gained in Sweden.

We had planned to join Berit's family for a Christmas - and New Year - holiday in Stockholm at the end of 1960. We made our way to Sweden via the north sea crossing from Harwich, and a long train journey from Holland through northern Europe. It was a tiring journey; but well worth it. For the first time I was able to celebrate a Swedish Christmas with Berit and her family: enjoying in particular the traditional customs of Julafton (Christmas Eve), when the main festive meal is served and Christmas gifts are distributed from under a candle-lit Christmas tree.

By the time I was due to return to London, Berit had begun to suspect that she had become pregnant; and in the days following my departure - when Berit stayed on in Stockholm for a further week - the early symptoms of morning sickness removed any doubt. Her return journey to England proved therefore an uncomfortable experience for her: the combination of rough sea and a more or less constant feeling of nausea would have made anybody feel ill-treated. When I met her at Liverpool Street station, she was near to the end of her tether: all delight at her starting a new family seemed to have vanished. We made our way home in a sombre spirit.

Back at home, however, Berit soon began to feel the eager anticipation of the prospective arrival of a new member of the family. This was reinforced by our GP's confirmation of the pregnancy; and his prediction that the baby would probably be born in the first week of September. As she was no longer employed, and we had taken on a lady to see to much of the household cleaning, Berit was able to devote much of her time to the many tasks of preparing for the new arrival. In particular, she was very conscientious in keeping to a routine of daily exercises, following the instruction provided by a Swedish gramophone record on "Modra gymnastic" (gymnastic exercises designed to ensure that pregnant women kept themselves in good physical shape). I have fond memories of Berit lying on her back doing cycling exercises with her feet pointing up to the ceiling!

As the months of 1961 slipped by,and Berit enjoyed a relatively untroubled pregnancy (apart from recurring symptoms of nausea which made the drinking of coffee and alcohol distasteful), we began to look forward to the birth with increasing confidence. But we had one important anxiety: the local maternity hospital had a policy that first births should be at home, attended by the midwife allocated to our care. Berit was doubtful about the wisdom of this policy, and felt she would be much happier to have the resources of a hospital available to her - just in case. For that reason, she decided to register with my mother's GP, who was in a position to command a place in the Woking Maternity Hospital. And it was there that Nicholas was born on 5 September. The custom of that time denied me the possibility of attending the birth: I had to wait anxiously in the corridor of the hospital until I could be admitted to the ward to welcome Nicholas, and to congratulate his mother. It was a joyful and reassuring moment: the babe gave every indication that he was very much alive!

*****

Several months before Nicholas arrived, I was moved from my second posting (where I was concerned with promoting employment opportunities for disabled people) to become Assistant Private

Secretary to the Minister of Labour. This appointment to the Minister's Private Office was not formally a promotion, but it carried an allowance on top of my salary as an AP, and was regarded by the Department as an important step towards promotion to Principal.

The role of a Minister's Private Office, and of the Private Secretaries, is essentially to ensure the best possible communication and understanding between the Minister and his most senior officials (and incidentally between the Department and the Prime Minister's office). On the one hand, this role requires officials to be fully informed of Cabinet and Ministerial decisions ; and on the other to ensure that official briefing of the Minister is timely, relevant and well considered. It calls for close and sympathetic rapport between Private Secretary and his or her Minister, and similarly diplomatic relations with senior officials, who need to be sensitive to the opinions of their Ministerial boss. Where politically important issues are emerging, and contentious matters affecting the Department are coming before the Cabinet, it often falls to the Private Secretary to ensure that discussion and briefing are adequate to enable the Minister to argue his case convincingly with his Cabinet colleagues. In short, the Minister's Private Office is the crucial transmission rod between the Ministerial drive and the Department's engine.

I was fortunate to be posted to the Minister of Labour's office after less than two years'service. I was even luckier that my boss, the Principal Private Secretary, was to be Kenneth Clucas. Ken was widely recognised to be one of the most capable officials in the Department; and his relationship with the Minister, John Hare, was exceptionally close and constructive. More important, from my point of view, Ken was a shrewd and supportive manager, who delegated much responsibility to his assistants and was always happy to acknowledge the contributions they made. Over the following five years, as I served under Ken in three quite different roles, I learned a great deal from him about what makes the ideal senior civil servant - and about how far I would have to develop to measure up to the standards Ken set!

(I also formed a close personal friendship with Ken and his family which lasted to his death in 2002).

The task of supporting a Minister naturally varies in detail with the character and ambitions of the person who holds the office; and with the political issues confronting the government and Department. John Hare was industrious and conscientious, but not very self-confident. We had often to reshape speeches and briefs supplied by officials, and to organize briefing meetings, in order to reassure him that he would not be thrown by awkward interventions by MP's. Moreover I would often find it necessary to redraft answers to Parliamentary Questions and to anticipate "Supplementary" Questions which MPs could be expected to raise. A major responsibility of the Private Secretary was to scrutinise briefing on matters coming to Cabinet, where several divisions in the Department had failed to highlight the key points the Minister should raise with his colleagues.

History will probably not credit John Hare as a very significant figure in the political firmament! He was not especially bright; and he was a bit of a bully to some of his officials, and did not therefore get the best from them. He was not a convincing performer in the House of Commons; and he needed a well prepared brief and much moral support from Ken Clucas to make any impact. But he had a conviction that the Ministry of Labour had much to do to fulfil its role in the difficult and rapidly changing economic environment of the latter years of the Macmillan government. Although he could not always define clearly what shifts in policy he believed were needed , he was astute enough to recognise the need for fresh initiatives in the fields of industrial training and industrial relations; and to put his weight behind ideas being shaped by his officials. His contribution to the government's plans for the reform of industrial training was important; and the passage of the Industrial Training Act, which was achieved after his move to become Chairman of the Conservative Party, owed much to Hare's promotion of this ambitious project. (An account, from my perspective, of its gestation, birth and development will form part of the next Chapter of this Memoir).

The arrival of Nicholas (as he was christened at a service in Pirbright Church in January 1962) not only gave us much joy, but brought home to us the limitations of our flat for an extension of our family. With our second bedroom becoming in effect a nursery, we would have little opportunity to welcome visitors for an overnight stay; nor would we easily accommodate any further additions to the family. Moreover, since the flat was two storeys up from the ground floor, and there was no lift in the building, it would be very inconvenient to lift a pram and other baby equipment to our floor. We had therefore been searching, before Nicholas was born, in a desultory way, for suitable alternative accommodation. Our quest was quickened in the early months of 1962 by two unexpected events. First, Ken and Barbara Clucas decided to acquire a building site in Godalming (having had a tipoff at a drinks party we hosted in autumn 1961) and to commission an architect to design a new house. Discussions with them (when business in the Minister's office was not too hectic!) about the opportunities of building a home for oneself spurred us to consider following their example. Secondly, in January 1962 we learned about a site for sale a mere four hundred metres from the Clucas's building plot; and at more or less the same time received from Berit's mother the gift of part of the legacy she (Margit) had inherited from her father . Our luck was in! We scarcely hesitated in making an offer for the site (at a cost of around £2000), despite our lack of any experience of the complexities of commissioning an architect and builder to create a new home to our specific requirements.

We fondly hoped that our architect would look after the problems of planning consent and negotiations with a reliable builder; we had only to satisfy ourselves that the building design met our key objectives. Over the following months we learned that it was not as simple as that. We had to take a multitude of decisions , often at short notice, on options of some technical complexity; and in urgent discussions with an architect who confessed that he had never before designed the type of timber-framed house he proposed for us! I well recall spending a significant part of our summer 1962 holiday on the island of Gotland poring over plans and specifications for our home-to-be, trying to imagine what would best meet our desires, at reasonable cost - so as to answer a number of questions the chosen architect, Paul White, had put to us.

We had hoped, and indeed expected, that the house would be ready for occupation by the end of 1962. We were indeed innocent! Work did not begin until the end of that year; and progress was then stalled by the onset of the most severe winter weather to hit the country since 1947. Sundry deadlines were posted - and then missed. We eventually moved in to Groton (as we had named our new home in honour of our Winthrop ancestors who were lords of the Manor of Groton) on American Independence Day 4 July 1964. It had been a long and testing journey. But we were delighted take possession of our very own home; and generally well satisfied with what had been achieved.

INDUSTRIAL TRAINING:
A NEW APPROACH

As I mentioned in the previous chapter, there was growing concern, within Government and the Ministry of Labour, in the early 60s, about the inadequacy of training arrangements to meet industry's requirements for skilled workers and to satisfy the aspirations of (especially) young people coming on to the labour market.

This concern was fuelled by four key considerations. First, poor training was identified in a number of reports as an important factor in the relatively lack-lustre economic performance of the country. Secondly, a lack of good quality training opportunities would gravely handicap the large number of young people, born in the immediate post-war years (" the Bulge"), who were coming on to the labour market in the 1960s. Thirdly, the great expansion in training undertaken by the government during the War years had not been maintained into the post war period, leaving a big gap in the output of skilled people. And, finally, there was much criticism of the quality of training provided for apprentices, which remained the major route to most skilled occupations.

In 1958, the Ministry of Labour's National Joint Advisory Committee published a report (usually referred to as the Carr Report, after Robert Carr, the Minister who chaired the Committee) drawing attention to these problems; and alerting employers to the pressing need to address them. It recommended the setting up of an Industry Training Council to spur action to widen training opportunities; but did not propose specific Government measures - beyond the development of technical colleges to expand the availability of technical education - to put direct pressure on employers and trade organisations to take up the challenge. Moves towards a bolder, interventionist Government approach were not entertained within the Macmillan government; and Ministers of Labour in the period up to 1960 did not believe that such intervention would attract sufficient support to gain industry's commitment.

This was broadly the position when I entered the Minister's (John Hare's) Private Office in the summer of 1961. However, I soon detected signs of a change of view within Government. One symptom of change was a growing conviction within the Treasury that a more activist economic policy was essential; and it was clear that the Prime Minister shared that view. Hare himself recognised that he needed to give a high priority to energising industry's approach to training; and instructed his senior officials to come up with ideas he could put to his Cabinet colleagues. Within the Ministry, moreover, there was considerable interest in the French Apprenticeship Levy. Could this be relevant, workable and acceptable within Britain? The Ministry decided to explore how the French system operated, and report back to the Minister.

At the same time as new ideas were being examined by Hare and his senior officials, the Government was moving to establish the National Economic Development Council (forever known as "Neddy") bringing together representatives of management, trades unions and Government in an attempt to address Britain's economic decline and stimulate action to achieve a significantly higher rate of economic growth. From this source would come pressure to review ways of improving the training output of the country.

By the middle of 1962, senior officials were working up options for a new approach. I well recall the "Eureka moment" when, at a conference organised by BACIE (the British Association for Commercial and Industrial Education) in 1962, Lady Gertrude Williams, Professor of Social Economics at London University (who was an expert on apprenticeship in Europe) advanced the idea of a training levy set at different rates on an industry-by industry basis. The idea struck an immediate chord with the Head of the Ministry's Training Division (Jim Stewart), who saw the potential for a scheme embracing a training levy administered by boards set up for individual industries.

By the end of 1962, John Hare had persuaded his Cabinet colleagues of the merits of this scheme; and his officials had drafted a White Paper outlining, for discussion with employers and trade unions, proposals for legislation that would empower the Minister to establish industry training boards (ITBs) with a range of responsibilities for promoting training and regulating standards of training within their respective industry sectors. Most importantly, the ITBs would have the power to raise a training levy from, and to pay training grants to, employers in their industry sectors. This "levy/grant system" was designed to increase the amount of training, and its quality while ensuring that all employers contributed to the cost.

The Cabinet endorsed these proposals and the White Paper was published at the end of 1962. It foreshadowed the most significant legislation in the manpower field since the end of the War.

I had no part, other than as a spectator, in securing this shift in the Government's manpower policy. But soon after the White Paper was published, I was promoted to head a small section in the Ministry of Labour's Training Division to take the lead in implementing the proposals. In essence, my responsibilities were to assist in carrying through the consultations with industry and education interests; contributing to the instructions to the legal draftsmen (Parliamentary Counsel) who would turn the proposals into legal form as a Bill; briefing the Minister on issues raised in consultations and on problems identified in the course of preparing the Bill; and drafting speeches for Ministers explaining the Government's thinking. I counted myself extremely fortunate to be involved in this initiative at its formative stage - the more so as my immediate boss would again be Ken Clucas, who had been the main author of the White Paper. I was sure that a post so close to the framing and execution of policy in a key manpower field, with frequent contacts with top officials and Ministers, must be the ideal opportunity for a newly promoted principal.

On a bitterly cold February day in 1963 I took my leave of the Permanent Secretary (whose private secretary I had been for the previous nine months), and arrived at my new office in Ebury Bridge Road: inconveniently distant from the Ministry's main offices in St James's Square. I had a single clerk in my section: no other staff! But Ken Clucas welcomed me warmly, and promised me that a competent Higher Executive officer would shortly be joining my section. We were quickly into discussions with the head of the Training Division, and with the Ministry's Legal Advisor about some of the detailed issues that we had to resolve before we could instruct the Parliamentary draftsmen. We also drew up a programme of consultations with employer and union representatives. My feet were quickly under the table - though I was uneasy about the magnitude of the project ahead of us.

The consultative process went very smoothly: employers and trades unions expressed relief that the Government was playing a more active role; and they supported the approach of progressing on an industry-by industry basis. They broadly welcomed the Government's decision to rely largely on industry bodies to take responsibility for shaping training --whilst granting the Boards the "muscle" to influence the actions of individual companies through a levy on employers. By the autumn of 1963, the Ministry was able to put before Parliament a Bill "for the purpose of making better provision for the training of persons over compulsory school age...". Then my main task was to ensure that Ministers were well prepared to deal with any issues raised in debate. This involved , among other things, sitting in the very cramped" Official Box" in the chamber of the House of Commons, ready to pass notes to the Minister on contentious points.

The Parliamentary debates on the Bill went extraordinarily smoothly. There was widespread agreement that this measure was necessary and timely. The main (Labour) opposition spokesman, Reg Prentice, urged the Government to "get on with it —and quickly"! The main issue raised was whether the Ministry of Labour would be sufficiently forceful in pressing for real changes in employer practice. It was therefore proposed that there should be an independent central body able to spur the Ministry to intervene when industry showed itself half-hearted in its approach. For that reason, the Government included in the Bill provision for a Central Training Council to advise the Minister on desirable improvements in the training system. It was hoped that this would bring pressure to bear on ITBs to embrace real reform.

Officials were sceptical that this would be necessary or desirable. They judged that the Minister would possess sufficient powers to influence ITBs(, whose levy/grant proposals and other training measures would require the approval of the Minister); and thought it doubtful whether the intervention of a central advisory body would be an effective addition to the Bill. Moreover Ministers felt it essential to emphasise the responsibility of individual industries to make the strategic decisions about training needs - and to pay for them! A central advisory body "second guessing" ITBs would not be consistent with the main thrust of the legislation. Nonetheless, the Minister agreed to bow to pressure - especially from the Trades Union Congress - to provide for a central advisory body.

One other aspect of the Bill attracted attention, and was a key objective for the Government: the integration into all training schemes of appropriate technical education, either in the form of "day release" (one day each week) or in blocks of formal instruction at a local technical college: in either case leading to a formal qualification and providing the possibility of broadening the trainee's skills. To further this objective, the legislation provided that there should be a representative of the further education service on every ITB; and that ITBs' training recommendations must include a further education element. The idea of thus integrating education and job training in a joint package was arguably the most significant influence the Government was to have under the new regime.

By the spring of 1964, the Bill had received Royal Assent; and attention turned to the substantial task of implementation: in particular setting up ITBs and the Central Training Council. This required the establishing, alongside my team, of two additional sections dedicated to securing agreement to the formation of ITBs in crucial sectors of the economy. Within the four years to 1968 more than a dozen ITBs were brought into existence: covering important manufacturing sectors (engineering, shipbuilding, chemicals, textiles, ceramics etc); the construction industry; printing; hotel and catering; retail distribution; and several textile sectors. In the main, employers and unions were positive about the new opportunities the legislation offered and were keen to see that their industries were not left behind. By the time I left the Training Division in 1968, I believed that an energetic start had been made in establishing the structure for a significant training advance - with some notable innovations in key industries. It helped that the Labour Government, elected in 1964, had committed itself to the introduction of a National Economic Plan with an economic growth target of 4% pa. The ITBs would be expected to gear themselves to making appropriate contribution towards this target.

My main responsibilities were to set up the Central Training Council, and help determine what role it could play in the new set up. I became the Secretary of the Council; and it was largely up to me to shape its Agenda in a way that would help it identify the contribution it could make. This was far from easy!

For a start, the CTC was an unwieldy body, with over twenty members - and a Chairman who, to put it kindly!, had few ideas to offer. It had no technical staff, who might help to develop ideas for discussion; and the Ministry had no plans to add to the Secretariat a cadre of experts (the Ministry appointed a single Chief Training Advisor whose task was ill defined but who was intended to provide guidance across the whole field of industry training). There was no research budget which would enable the Council to develop fresh initiatives. Above all, the Ministry was not in a mood to give any priority to an additional and, possibly, "wayward" unit that might cut across the lines of accountability between the Ministry and the ITBs.

After some desultory attempts to identify areas for study (I recall that we assembled a set of general guidelines about the use of teaching machines in training new recruits), I put forward a case for producing a report on the training of office and clerical staff who were to be found in every industry - and who were likely to be overlooked by ITBs focused on the specific skills required in their industries. The proposal was well received . I was invited to set up a small committee to take this forward; and I set about finding a group of people who were sufficiently knowledgeable to add something of real value to the Ministry's policy-making and ITBs' thinking.

Over the period 1965/66, much of my time was devoted to the Commercial and Clerical Training Committee, whose chairman, Joe Hunt (a prominent West Midlands industrialist, who was very committed to improving training standards) gave me a great deal of encouragement and support.

The Committee met a number of companies with experience of making best use of office staff. I also led a small group on a study tour of Germany, France and Denmark to glean ideas about the organisation of office training in these countries. Towards the end of 1966, we had compiled a report which contained some principles of general application in all companies; a summary of the lessons we drew from the experience in the other European countries we had visited; and a proposal for a new form of off-the-job training and further education,which could be adapted to the different needs of different companies (and which, we believed, could best be delivered in colleges of further education, which had excellent ties with their local firms). The report was warmly endorsed by the Central Training Council; and published in 1966 (It was presented to the press by the recently appointed junior minister at the Ministry, Shirley Williams, in her first Ministerial post).

I hoped that this initiative might serve as a model for the future work of the CTC. But I feared that it would prove difficult for the Council to achieve a significant impact because of the problems I have referred to above. And so, I think, it proved. By the time I moved to a new post in 1967, it would be difficult to argue that the Council had made much headway.

******

How successful did the Industrial Training Act prove in achieving the advances in training output, quality and commitment which we hoped for in the early sixties? Surprisingly little independent research by universities and other organisations or individuals has been carried out to provide a satisfactory answer to this question. The most recent study I have been able to unearth was a PhD thesis by Hugh Pemberton, whose conclusion(published in 2001) was that the Act had proved to be "a failed revolution". Pemberton argues that the Act "failed to disturb significantly prevailing attitudes towards training or reforming apprenticeship". He put this down to a weak central council and the inability of the Ministry of Labour to "prevail over the fragmentation of institutions operating in the labour market" . He judged that the Government hesitated to push ahead aggressively for fear of disturbing relationships with industry . His overall conclusion was that the Act was " a gamekeepers charter"! However, he advanced little hard evidence from an examination of data on employers' attitudes, training numbers or innovations by ITBs etc that might serve to support this bleak assessment .

It was my fate to be plunged into the first major review of the Act when, in 1979, I was appointed Chief Executive of the Manpower Service Commission's Training Division.

By that time there were fundamental changes - political,economic and statutory - in the environment in which the ITBs operated.

The Conservative Government, under Edward Heath, had decided in the early 1970s to set up the Manpower Services Commission to manage and finance the employment and training services that had hitherto been part of the Ministry of Labour (or Department of Employment as it became). The idea was that operational and management efficiency would be improved if these agencies were not under direct Ministerial control, and had a larger degree of independence. One important consequence of this change was that the ITBs came under the supervision of the Commission and its Training Division; and there was established within that Division a greatly expanded Directorate to strengthen contacts with the ITBs.

A second change in the 1970s was a growing wariness (and weariness) among employers about Government attempts to "manage" industry. This was epitomised by the antagonism towards the industrial policies promoted by Tony Benn; but it also reflected increasing scepticism about the capacity of Governments to develop economic strategies to achieve efficiency and growth. The election of a Conservative government under Margaret Thatcher in 1979 reinforced that scepticism - and indeed challenged many of the policies of the preceding decades - including the role of ITBs.

Thirdly, the performance of the ITBs was seen to be patchy, over-involved in the details of training within employers' establishments, and imposed costs which some employers regarded as excessive. After fifteen years' experience of the IT Act, many felt it was time to have a hard look at what the —often complex--levy/grant system had achieved. This chimed with the new Government's instincts.

By the time I had settled into my new seat, the Secretary of State, James Prior, had signalled clearly to the MSC that he expected the Commission to undertake a fundamental review of the ITBs - and quickly. This review was to become my main preoccupation for the next 2 years; and the fate of individual ITBs was to be partly in my hands: a very uncomfortable prospect!

In one respect, the review provided a good opportunity for me , as the incoming Chief Executive, to take a cool look at the relations of the ITBs to the MSC, and of the relations of the ITBs to their industries. Had the timetable been more realistic, I would have chosen to commission an independent unit to carry out a survey of the views of industry and to provide hard evidence of the performance and impact of ITBs. But when I took up my new post the Commission had already decided that the review should be in the hands of my Division in order to bring a report back within the shortest possible time. In retrospect this was an unhappy decision - even if it was politically inevitable.

One other aspect of the review made the exercise awkward for me. The report was to be rendered to the Manpower Services Commission; but its real destination was Ministers' desks. Within the Commission there might well be marked differences between the employers and Trade union representatives; but one could be sure that Ministers would expect a markedly cool assessment of the ITB performance and usefulness. How could I best serve the two masters?

The Commission set up a Working Group, with similar representation to the Commission itself, and under its Chairman (Sir Richard O'Brien), to supervise the Review and give me and my staff guidance on the scope and emphasis of the Review. It took us a while to work out a realistic approach to a complex assignment; and I found it necessary to change key staff, and to involve myself more closely in the detailed drafting than I expected. After the better part of a year what emerged was a report that underlined the potential benefits of the levy/grant system: if applied by ITBs in an efficient manner, with good lines of constructive communication with their industries and a soundly based set of priorities. This conclusion was accompanied by a recommendation that a second stage of the Review should assess the performance of individual Boards against the criteria we had set down.

The Commission endorsed this (conditional) conclusion; and the Secretary of State, Mr James Prior, accepted it in principle, subject to a thorough investigation of every ITB.

Here was the rub! It was necessary to require the staff in my Division who were responsible for supervising the ITBs to undertake , in addition to their ongoing tasks, a robust and defensible assessment of the performance of the Boards they supervised,, taking full account of the often different views of employers and unions - in next to no time! In many cases my staff had established cordial and trusted relations with "their" ITB; and it went against the grain for them to become judge and jury in assessing whether the Board should survive.

We did our best to establish sensible objective measures of ITB performance. But there was no way of avoiding some uncertain and uncomfortable judgements, and apparently ill-supported comparisons between ITBs. My predecessor, who had resigned from the Civil Service to join the private sector, described the whole process as "a Micky Mouse exercise"! He may have had a point; but politics is often conducted according to rules and procedures that defy logic and justice! It was the most unsatisfactory passage in my career; and I was left with the responsibility of signing off the assessment of each ITB, often involving an implied recommendation for a Board to be axed.

When my report came to be considered by the Commission (happily on the final day of the crucial Third Test match between England and Australia in July 1981, which drew attention away from controversial issues!), the Chairman and Director-General of the Commission and I were faced with the inevitable disagreement between employer and trade union members about the line to take on the future of some ITBs.

We proposed a classic fudge! In those industries where there was general support for the continuation of the ITB, the Commission agreed to recommend accordingly. In other cases, the Commission agreed that more work would be required to reach a firm decision. In effect, the matter was left to the Secretary of State to decide!

James Prior was happy to have the opportunity, without open dissent from the Commission, to decide the fate of ITBs. His Department quickly set about disbanding the ITBs about which the MSC had expressed uncertainty; and for good measure included one or two the Commission wished to retain. Within a very few years, almost the sole "survivors" were the Engineering Industry Training Board (EITB) and the Construction Industry Training Board (CITB): always the industries that were judged by the Government to be crucial to the supply of skilled workers and apprenticeship opportunities. The "experiment" of legislating for the improvement of training through a levy/grant system was largely at an end: except that, to this day, the EITB and CITB survive!

Looking back over these events, I have two questions: could I have secured a different outcome? What damage was done by the apparently cavalier way that the Department of Employment set about dismantling the machinery put in place by the Industrial Act, nearly twenty years earlier?

As to the first question, with hindsight I think I might have pressed for a more fundamental independent examination of the impact of the ITBs on training numbers and standards etc. But I doubt whether I would have been successful in the face of the political pressures from the incoming Conservative Government. At all events, I recognised that a decision had been taken before my arrival on the scene.

As to the consequences of the abolition of most ITBs, I have following reflections:

The ITBs were being dismantled, and their staffs made redundant at precisely the period (1981 to 1984) when youth unemployment was threatening to go through the roof. The Government was being forced to introduce an emergency scheme - the Youth Training Scheme - to provide, at much greater expense to the Exchequer than the cost of maintaining the ITBs-- a large number of temporary job opportunities for the young unemployed. It seems to me that many of the ITBs, if retained, would have been well placed to contribute to the Government's scheme a valuable training element.

Secondly, however, it is fair to observe that the notable expansion of College and university places that was taking place from the 1970's onwards did offer many ambitious and able young people an alternative to traditional apprenticeships, which mitigated to some extent the falling off of training places the ITBs may have financed.

Third, the country was fortunate that the greatly increased immigration of skilled people from EU countries from the late 1980s made up for some of the shortfall in skilled training by British employers - especially in construction, agriculture, the entertainment sectors and in hospitals and other public services (and of course in Premier League football!). That infusion may now be reduced by Brexit, leaving the country more dependent on home grown training. But it has in the past twenty or more years helped to supply the skills needed .

Fourth, it was inescapable that many training experts nurtured by the ITBs, among their own staff and in companies with approved training arrangements, were dispersed and often lost to industry. Moreover , it is likely that the incentives for companies to invest in training will have been weakened by the ending of the training levy: especially at a time of rising unemployment and recession in the early 1980s.

I left the training scene somewhat despondent about the future; and the years after my departure did not increase my optimism. One reason I felt pessimistic was that I could see the possibility that, as the Government dismantled most of the ITB's, it also raised questions about the future of the MSC itself. If the Commission had no continuing role to supervise and energise the ITBs, and no resources to add power to its responsibility, could it exercise a genuinely independent influence on national training policies? Whilst the Commission largely designed and managed the major programmes providing emergency youth employment and training opportunities from 1982, these were financed entirely by the Government - and in the last resort the Government would decide on their shape and extent in the light of the political realities they faced. The Commission would do as the Government wished! And in that case, what was the argument for a quasi-independent Council to remain in existence? I did not have to address that question before I left the Commission's service at the end of 1982 ; but I could see it looming.

A GROWING FAMILY IN THE SIXTIES

Before I move on to a later stage in my career as a civil servant, it is time to devote more attention to my life as a family man.

Before we moved to Godalming, we welcomed Andrew to our family; and the boys acquired a little sister, Karin, in August 1966. It only required the arrival of a Dalmatian puppy, Katja, to complete the family circle. We were delighted that our new home would be fully occupied; and that we had three healthy and active children to share our lives.

We moved in to Groton (as we christened our home in honour of the Winthrop connection with the Manor of Groton in the Sixteenth and Seventeenth centuries) on the Fourth of July 1964. By happy coincidence this was American Independence Day.

The house had, downstairs, a generous sized living room, with an open fireplace; a kitchen and utility space; and a further room which we intended to serve as a breakfast room and playroom. Upstairs there were four bedrooms and a single bathroom. We planned that the smallest room, next to our bedroom, would be suitable for the youngest member of the family; and that the boys would share one of the larger bedrooms - leaving the fourth bedroom for the occasional guest.

Outside we had a half acre of garden, which would provide plenty of play space for the children (and Katja!). One side of the site was fringed by a row of about forty mature elms, which Nicholas soon turned into his climbing den. The lower part of the garden sloped fairly steeply down to a wooded area, but had plenty of space for a sandpit, swing and wooden climbing frame. The upper garden would be planted with a shrub border, fringed by a substantial lawn.

Beyond the house, Godalming offered easy access to an attractive countryside with an almost limitless number of public spaces for walking. There was also a good range of local schools to choose from when the kids reached the age to start school.

We were not sad to leave behind the densely populated metropolis, and to swop it for the amenities of a relatively small market town.

We soon gathered and got to know well a number of good friends. In this we benefited from the fact that Ken and Barbara Clucas had moved to Godalming a year ahead of us; and they introduced us to many of their circle of friends. We also got to know a number of members of a "Town and Gown" discussion group which met monthly and brought together Charterhouse teachers and (mainly) members of local churches.

In addition, Berit soon got to know other young mums through her contacts with several play and pre-school groups, which we judged suitable for Nicholas.

It did not therefore take us long to feel settled and happy with the choice and timing of our move from London. We felt that we could focus very happily on giving our children the best possible start in their lives.

Our general approach to parenting could best be summed up as: Firm but fair,with fun and much affection. Much has been written about the supposed new freedoms and permissive culture of the so-called "Swinging sixties" and the changed attitudes towards child rearing (among many other social changes) that these years encouraged. But we - as, I suspect, most other couples - tried to combine the virtues of a traditional emphasis on "good behaviour" with warmth and openness (which may often have been missing from many families in previous generations). Our children may sometimes have felt that we were unduly strict and unyielding; but they mainly accepted the limits we set (and they knew it was no good appealing to one of the parents against the ruling of the other!) And, most important, they always knew that they were loved and never condemned.

Inevitably I was less closely involved in the management of the family than was Berit, because I usually returned home from my work in London after the children had had supper, been bathed, and put to bed. She therefore tended to set the tone of much family life: including discipline. Though I shared her views on virtually all matters touching the children, it was usually she who had to take the day-to-day decisions about the ordering of family life. I greatly admired the consistency and fairness she invariably showed, as well as the loving warmth. And as the children grew older, she was very ready to allow them a - perhaps surprising - freedom to do their own thing.

We established early in these pre-school years the practice of holidaying every other summer in Sweden. The pattern we followed was to rent a country cottage (usually by a lake or near the Baltic coast) for a fortnight and then drive to Stockholm to spend a week or so meeting up with Berit's relations and friends - and enjoying outings to Skansen, Grona Lund or to islands in the Stockholm Archipelago. Berit's mother Margit (known to all the family as Mimi) frequently joined us for our stay in the country cottage. This cemented the strong affection which grew between her and our children. Back in Stockholm we could often find accommodation in the home of Berit's aunt Gerd and her husband Lasse.

In my account books (holidays always cost money!) I have noted that, over the sixties and seventies, we rented cottages in Sodermanland, Smaland (at least twice), Dalarna, Halsingland, Dalsland and Skane, and spent a fortnight in a Pension in Gryts Skargard on the Baltic coast south of Stockholm. We never failed to enjoy these holiday breaks; and (in our recollection) the sun always shone!

I have especially fond memories of our stay in a cottage in Dalarna, overlooking Lake Siljan,in 1971. On this occasion Berit's brother Jan and his family rented the cottage next to ours; and our children and his spent many happy hours playing together. It was perhaps this experience which led us to consider moving permanently to

Sweden: though, as I have explained in the previous chapter, we did not quite take the plunge.

Needless to say, these Swedish holidays served to reinforce the strong attachment which all three of our children felt towards their Swedish heritage and their Swedish relatives (which have lasted to this day). In these formative years - roughly from 1963/4 to the end of the sixties decade - the selection of schools for the children often preoccupied our family planning. Few play schools on the Swedish model were established in Godalming - and certainly none provided at public expense. We were driven to settle on private play schools (which were more like schools than play groups) to give the children the opportunity of preparing, socially and academically, for the start of "real" school at 5 years old.

The big question then was: what school should we select when the children reached their fifth birthday?

After much thought - and many discussions with friends with offspring of similar age - we settled on the small village primary school at Shackleford a mile or two outside Godalming, rather than one of the more local schools. I do not recall precisely what determined this choice. We were certainly impressed by the headmaster, Mr Kinnear, who struck us as humane and keen to move with the times - and was keen to widen the range of pupils beyond the children of "the village folk". We were also aware that the teacher of the entry class was regarded as a "progressive". The class sizes were relatively small: partly because there were not a large number of village children of school age. But what struck us most was the friendly atmosphere encouraged by the head and his teaching staff.

Nicholas entered Shackleford school very shortly after his fifth birthday in September 1966 - and he thrived there for most of the following 4 years. He was fortunate that his first teacher, Ella Henderson, was an inspiring and imaginative individual who brought out the best in all her pupils: both the ablest and those who needed a lot of support. Nicholas responded to Ella's encouragement, and proved himself an apt pupil, always scoring high marks for achievement and diligence. But in his last year he came under the negative influence of a teacher who had largely lost interest in her vocation, and was looking for quiet and submissive pupils to people her class in the last year before she retired . Nicholas did not fit this requirement! He lost a good deal of his motivation. After some soul-searching, we concluded that he would be dragged down further if he stayed on at Shackleford; and that he would benefit more from entry to Haslemere Heights Preparatory School. This could prepare him for entry to a public school in due course, if he did not succeed in the 11 plus exam and gain entry to the Grammar School .

Nicholas was an able and industrious pupil who set high standards for himself. He fitted in well to the more challenging academic environment of the Heights; and he did very well in all subjects. But when the opportunity came to test himself against the general population in the 11 Plus, he took his chance and won selection to Godalming Grammar School.

The pattern of schooling for Andrew and Karin was somewhat similar to Nicholas'. They enjoyed three years at Shackleford before we felt they should move on to private schools where they would be more challenged. So Andrew followed Nicholas to Haslemere Heights, while Karin moved to St Hilary's School in Godalming: in both cases with the expectation that they would continue in the private sector until at least they reached the sixth form after taking their O Level exams.

It is clear from what I have written above that, in these years of the sixties, our lives were inevitably focused on the development of the children; and that we were very happy that it should be so. Apart from holidays and schooling, the kids came to enjoy walking - often with Katja alongside - in the countryside around Godalming; they learned to swim at the ancient Charterhouse baths under the authoritarian supervision of Danny, an instructor on the Charterhouse staff; they enjoyed a succession of birthday parties (home and Away); and they learned to cycle around the local roads, not yet as crowded as they have since become.

At home, the children spent a good deal of their time watching a clutch of lively Television programmes that were being produced (mainly) by the BBC for the younger audience: notably Magic Roundabout and Blue Peter; and later Dr Who and Thunderbirds. Bedtime seldom passed without the reading of a story, often from Swedish authors like Astrid Lindgren (who wrote of Pippi Longstocking, a bold, mischievous and energetic girl who set a "naughty" example to her friends and readers).

It was, in the main, a relatively comfortable and unfrightening introduction to the world in which they would grow up.

******

Looking back on the key years of the "Swinging Sixties" (broadly the period between the election of the Labour Government in 1964 and its defeat six years later in the 1970 election), I find it surprising to recall that my sharpest memories are of the gritty and negative realities of social and political life rather than the "swinging". Surprising because our family life and progress seemed so happy; and because much of the public perception of these years was generally optimistic and positive.

Certainly there were many things to welcome and enjoy in these years. The steady growth in earnings for those in employment and the enormous increase in house and car ownership gave a strong sense of achievement to many millions. There was a greater openness to discussion about sex---and enjoyment of it (prompted to some degree by the arrival of the contraceptive Pill in 1961). The advance of the supermarket made household shopping easier and more fun. And the Miniskirt - and the Mini car-- were everywhere, at least in the main metropolitan centres (it was said that the Mini skirt was not seen in Hull and Sunderland until the late sixties!).

In addition, these were the years of the Beatles. Between 1963 and 1967, the Beatles, according to Dominic Sandbrook in " White Heat", his history of the sixties, "completely reshaped the contours of popular music, not only defining what popular music was, but completely challenging the tastes of their audience... No other group better captured the sound and spirit of the 60s". (I have to confess that I only discovered the Beatles after they produced Sergeant Pepper; but I was far behind most of the population under the age of 30!).

And yet... What struck me most forcefully about the period is best illustrated by two events which presented a rather different picture of the reality of life for many who were not in a position to shop in Carnaby Street or holiday in Benidorm.

The first of these events was the BBC's production of the TV play "Cathy Come Home" in December 1966. This play, directed by Ken Roach, was one of the series of Wednesday Plays produced by the BBC's drama department from 1964, intended to address controversial social issues and to give prominence to working class characters. "Cathy" traced the descent of a working class couple into homelessness, poverty and despair, until Cathy's children were received into the care of singularly unsympathetic social workers. I remember watching the programme and being shaken by its honesty and directness. It illustrated sharply the way in which homelessness destroyed a family which was in no sense to blame for its fate. And it was soon followed by documentary programmes and research which cast a similarly critical eye on the unhappy situation of many elderly pensioners left lonely, frail, and in desperate housing conditions by a society which seemed unaware or complacent about these problems.

Even today, fifty years on from Cathy, we can scarcely assert that we have got the measure of the problems highlighted by this TV play.

The second event happened while I was in hospital for the extraction of an impacted wisdom tooth on 19/20 November 1967. As I came round from the anaesthetic, I heard that the government had just announced the decision to devalue the pound against the dollar by about 14%. This decision was taken after unavailing attempts to deal with the rapidly growing imbalance between imports and exports (the trade balance) and a fear that, without devaluation, there would be an uncontrollable run on the pound and little hope that international institutions would be ready to "bail us out".

At that time, I was writing a pamphlet of guidance to employers (and Unions) about Company manpower planning, as a modest contribution to the Government's economic strategy, the National Economic Plan. I was quickly seized of the obvious consequence: the Economic Plan was dead in the water; and the Government's strategy was in ruins. Though the Prime Minister did his best to assure the country that "the pound in your pocket" is unaffected, the Chancellor of the Exchequer, James Callaghan acknowledged the truth in a sober and honest statement to the House of Commons - and promptly resigned his post.

In an important sense, the devaluation was a humiliating reverse for the Labour Government, since nobody could fail to see that the ringing confidence that the Labour Government had shown in 1964 had vanished. As Dominic Sandbrook put it: "As 1967 drew to a close, there was a palpable sense that the optimism and glamour of the mid-sixties had disappeared. The politicians who had once been the heralds of optimism... had now become the harbingers of woe... It was as though, after the intoxication of the swinging years, the country was paying the price for its pleasures."

The Government would have an immensely difficult task to recover its morale and reputation before the next election; and I was to find myself, in a new post, deeply involved in that task. That is the burden of the next chapter. (In the meantime, my pamphlet on Company Manpower Planning was published by the Ministry of Labour's Manpower Research Unit early in 1968!).

IN PLACE OF STRIFE

Throughout the Sixties there was a groundswell of criticism of the disorderly character of industrial relations. Much of this criticism was focused on the number, and seriousness, of so-called "wildcat strikes": industrial action pursued without the authority or agreement of a trade union, and often in breach of agreements between employers and trade unions. However, despite the evidence of days lost to industrial disputes (in the period 1964 to 1967 there were on average over 2000 strikes each year .involving the loss of well over 2 million working days), successive governments were extremely cautious about committing themselves to introducing legislation to regulate relations between employers and unions or to penalise or restrain strikers.

When the Labour Party was returned to power after thirteen years of Conservative government, in 1964, the Wilson government was also cautious about proposing legislation that might be seen as anti-trade union. The newly appointed Minister of Labour, Ray Gunter, therefore, decided to appoint a Royal Commission to inquire into the system of collective UK labour law, and to recommend what should be done to improve industrial relations. The Commission was chaired by a distinguished Appeal Court Judge, Lord Donovan, who had extensive political and industrial experience; and included senior employer and trade union representatives as well as influential academics in the field of labour law.

The Commission reported in 1968. It disappointed expectations that it would favour significant new powers for the government to deal with industrial disputes. It was profoundly sceptical about the efficacy or desirability of giving governments powers to intervene in collective bargaining. Its main recommendation, in favour of setting up an Industrial Relations Commission to promote improved procedural arrangements and agreements between employers and unions, was widely seen as a "cop out" . It would do little to deal with unofficial strikes or inter-union disputes. There was much pressure on the government to go beyond the Donovan prescription: the catchword was "Donovan Plus".

Prime Minister Wilson quickly saw an opportunity for the Government to seize the initiative, and regain some of its lost authority, by introducing bolder legislation. He hoped that this would reassure the public that a Labour government was capable of tackling what were seen as the major symptoms of disorder in the conduct of industrial relations.

His first step was to promote Barbara Castle, a left-leaning politician who had made a name for herself as a reforming Minister of Transport, to become - as she would be called - First Secretary of State and Secretary of State for Employment and Productivity. He charged her with responsibility for designing legislation that would bring new order to industrial relations - and "dish the Tories". Both her title and her mission indicated clearly that her status in the Cabinet, and her new Department's in Whitehall, would be greatly increased.

Barbara Castle was well aware of the problems she would face in confronting the trade union movement with the threat of legal restraints and sanctions; but she was convinced that a balanced set of measures offering significant benefits to unions and employees could attract a wide measure of support from moderate trade union leaders and members, who were often as sickened by wildcat strikes as the general public. She was, by temperament and conviction, an activist who saw clearly the need for a bold and determined initiative to change the culture of industrial relations.

Her instincts chimed with the views of her most senior officials, who had long been persuaded that the government should adopt a more interventionist approach than had characterised previous post-war administrations led by Clement Attlee, Winston Churchill and Harold Macmillan (and their Ministers of Labour).

As a first step in testing what measures were essential to shape a new culture, Barbara Castle decided to hold a weekend conference at the Civil Service College at Sunningdale, where she would assemble a range of officials, personal advisers and a handful of industry and trade union representatives to explore a package that would offer a convincing and balanced new approach to the issues that Donovan was judged to have failed to tackle.

It was at this juncture that I appeared on the scene, and was plunged into the political and legislative turmoil of the period from 1968 to 1973. I was posted from the Department's Manpower Research Unit to become an additional Private Secretary to the Secretary of State. This was not a promotion, but it carried an allowance in recognition of the additional working hours it would certainly entail. My role was to lend support to the Principal Private Secretary, Douglas Smith, who had already established himself as an outstanding and notably adroit and sympathetic aide for Barbara Castle. I was also to strengthen the management of the Private Office, and to play a part in ensuring good communication between officials involved in preparing the industrial relations legislation and the Secretary of State (and Downing Street).

I had no direct responsibility at this point for developing the main strands of policy. But I became immediately involved in organising the conference at Sunningdale in November 1968; and thereafter in the work of Barbara's Private Office that followed the Conference, and led on to debates in Cabinet and with the Trades Union Congress (TUC).

My first extensive exposure to Barbara Castle's way of doing business was at the Sunningdale conference. She was decidedly energetic and very much engaged in all the discussions that took place. She struck up good rapport with the various outside representatives; and listened attentively to the ideas they put forward. She drew people into debate in a way that made them feel listened to. But it was clear from the outset that she had formed some firm ideas of her own, which she wanted to test.

We all felt the force of her personality - and would later come to think of her as a latter-day Tudor Monarch (The flaming red hair and her political courage invited comparison with Queen Elizabeth I!). At the end of two full days of discussion, she had a clear view, which those present supported with enthusiasm and conviction, of the key strands of policy she would want to present to her Cabinet colleagues. She felt that the conference had well served her purposes; and increased her confidence about the way forward. It was now for officials to draw the threads together in a draft White Paper, which she could put to Cabinet soon after Christmas.

The White Paper was ready for submission to Cabinet by Christmas. It bore the title "In Place of Strife"(which had been suggested by Barbara's husband Ted to bring to the minds of Labour stalwarts the pamphlet "In Place of Fear" written some years earlier by the left wing hero Aneurin Beavan). It proposed a balanced set of measures which it was hoped would appeal to trade unionists (including the right to belong to a union and procedures designed to assist unions seeking recognition from employers) and powers for the government to intervene in unofficial disputes which threatened serious damage to the economy .

After assuring herself of Harold Wilson's agreement and enthusiastic support, Barbara circulated the draft to some senior ministers before it was formally presented to the Cabinet for debate in January.

Unhappily, the draft was leaked to the Trades Union Congress (TUC), enabling it to alert , among others, James Callaghan to trade union opposition to the so-called "penal clauses", which would restrain trade union action and possibly land trade union members in jail. When the Cabinet came to consider the White Paper, therefore, Callaghan urged caution on his colleagues. After considerable, and often heated, debate over several meetings, the cabinet approved the publication of the White Paper in late January. But it was already evident that a smooth passage for the legislation was very uncertain.

The White Paper was well received in the press; and in Barbara's whirlwind tour of trade union meetings during the winter months she found a wide measure of support and agreement for her proposals. But within the TUC, and among its leading union officials(especially Jack Jones of the Transport Workers union and Hugh Scanlon of the Engineers) the resistance to the Government's proposals for intervening in unofficial strikes and inter-union disputes became ever more forceful. And the TUC's concerns were taken seriously by a strong body of Labour MPs, whose support for the legislation was essential if it was to reach the Statute Book.

This was the situation which confronted me when, in January 1969, I was promoted (to the rank of Assistant Secretary**) to head a Branch of the Industrial Relations Division which was to take responsibility for drafting the proposed legislation and advising ministers on key issues to which the legislation gave rise.

** One of the curiosities of Civil Service terminology on grades is that to the outsider the more senior the rank the less authority its title appeared to enjoy! Thus the move up from Principal was to Assistant Secretary. And if one was lucky enough to progress from there, it was to Under Secretary, Deputy Secretary and, ultimately Permanent Secretary.

I was thus in a prime position to observe, and very occasionally to influence, the course of events during the winter and spring when the Government sought to secure sufficient support from the Cabinet and the Labour Party to frame legislation that hopefully would be applauded by the general public and be acceptable to the trade unions (and more specifically the TUC General Council).

The course of events in the period from January to June 1969 has nowhere been better recorded than in an (unpublished) Memoir by my former Permanent Secretary Sir Conrad Heron, who was a key player in the increasingly fractious dialogue between Barbara Castle and the TUC. I saw only glimpses of this struggle at first hand. I am therefore attaching to this Memoir Conrad Heron's masterly record, which brings out clearly the falling support in Cabinet for the legislation in the face of the TUC's unforgiving opposition to any government powers to halt industrial action in unofficial and inter-union disputes.

By the early summer, Harold Wilson and Barbara Castle were driven to seeking the best assurance they could from the TUC that they (the TUC) would undertake to deal effectively with damaging disputes. The TUC offered to the deflated Ministers what came to be called a "Solemn and Binding Undertaking" to use its authority to resolve disputes between their member unions. In return, the Government agreed to suspend its proposed arrangements for dealing with strikes.

The government claimed this "Undertaking" as an historic breakthrough! But few were deceived! It was widely regarded as a humiliating defeat for the Government and, more particularly, for Barbara Castle herself. Though she continued to pursue the preparation of a modest bill, shorn of any mention of "penal clauses" and "conciliation pauses", it would never see the light of day: the Labour Government was voted out of office in the General Election of 1970 before the alternative bill reached the House of Commons.

It was impossible for my Branch to make much progress in drafting a bill to implement "In Place of Strife" in the absence of any agreement on the most fundamental issues. In these circumstances, I spent a good deal of my time preparing notes on the main arguments Ministers could advance in negotiations with the TUC. I recall, in particular, struggling to show that the proposed legislation to restrain unofficial strikes need not - and should not - result in sending strikers to prison. The law should be drafted to provide only financial penalties. If a striker refused to pay, there would be provision for the courts to make an order to require his employer to subtract the fine from his pay packet (a procedure known as "attachment of earnings"). All my instincts told me that this would only inflame debate; and I advised accordingly. Perhaps it was as well that we never reached a point to test my instinct!

One consequence of the demise of Barbara Castle's plans - apart from her personal loss of standing in the Labour Party - was that it paved the way for, and in a sense made inevitable, Conservative legislation to pursue many of the objectives of "In Place of Strife".

******

The incoming Conservative government, led by Edward Heath and with Robert Carr as Minister of Labour, lost no time in following up its manifesto commitment to reform industrial relations. The Conservatives had already set out their stall in a pamphlet entitled "A Fair Deal at Work", published at about the same time as the Donovan Report. This had been drafted mainly by Conservative lawyers rather than people with extensive practical experience of dealing with trades unions. But it had attracted fairly general support among Tory MPs and it provided the government with an agreed basis for its legislative programme.

Rather like a second act of a dramatic play, Robert Carr soon followed Barbara Castle's example by convening a weekend conference at Sunningdale. This time the dramatis personae were largely confined to senior officials; and there was little questioning the direction the government would be steering. Carr was a genial chairman, who had the benefit of previous experience as a junior minister in the Ministry of Labour. He quickly steered discussion to the key topics the legislation should address; and his officials (including myself) felt that he gave us the lead we needed - and wanted. It was, in my recollection, a relaxed meeting, all the more reassuring because we felt that the work done in support of In Place of Strife would not be entirely wasted. My Branch and I would be clear what was required; and confident that there would be the support in the House of

Commons (and in the Lords for that matter) for the main features of the legislation.

Carr's personality and experience favoured, like Barbara Castle, a balanced package which could appeal both to unions and employers. Though he was well aware of the likely hostility of the TUC, he hoped that the outcome of the election would modify union opposition and offer hope of a more rational "give and take" approach.

What emerged from Sunningdale —and was subsequently quickly endorsed by Cabinet - was what Carr described as " the Seven Pillars". According to my recollection these could be summarized as follows:

• The right to belong, and not to belong, to a trade union;
• The presumption that collective agreements would be legally enforceable
• Measures to enable trade unions to secure recognition from unwilling employers, where the union had support in the company or factory
• Emergency powers for the Government to intervene in strikes of national importance, and to require a strike ballot before industrial action was embarked on
• Recourse to industrial tribunals by employees who felt they were unfairly dismissed
• The (voluntary) registration of employers associations and trade unions
• The setting up of a National Industrial Relations Court to deal with issues arising out of the legislation.

This was a formidable Agenda; and if passed would represent the most fundamental change in the legal framework of industrial relations since the early 1900s. It would fall to my Branch to assume the major share of responsibility for bringing the measures to the statute book.

The team of senior officials, under my immediate boss John Burgh, appointed to prepare instructions to Parliamentary Council (the Government's professional legal draftsmen) was greatly reinforced and energised by the appointment of Sir Geoffrey Howe (newly appointed as Solicitor General, who had responsibility for advising the Government on all civil law issues) as our Ministerial guide. He had spent much time as a senior barrister dealing with legal cases arising from industrial disputes; made a significant contribution to the ideas in "Fair Deal at Work; and for good measure had studied North American legislation, which was in some respects a model for "Fair Deal".

Sir Geoffrey was a delight to work with. I have very happy memories of sitting round John Burgh's table in St James's Square swopping ideas about the trickier issues, assessing the likely reactions of employers and unions, and the practical problems we had to resolve. Geoffrey brought to these discussions an incisive mind, a keen sense of humour and a lack of personal vanity. He was very comfortable with officials; and because Robert Carr delegated much responsibility to Geoffrey, his role made for the ideal means of combining ministerial and official contributions to the shaping of the legislation.

One key element of collaboration was notably missing. The TUC refused absolutely to engage in any discussion of the legislation, either with ministers or officials. The only meeting with TUC representatives was called by Robert Carr soon after Cabinet had endorsed the legislative proposals. At this meeting Carr outlined the main proposals the Government intended to enact; and he invited the TUC to engage with the Department in examining some of the detailed matters that would arise. The TUC, led by its General Secretary Victor Feather, would have none of it. If the government were not prepared to abandon any of its "Pillars", there could be no fruitful dialogue. The TUC had successfully fought the Labour government on their "conciliation pause" proposals; and saw no point in parleying with the Conservatives who were intent on pushing ahead with similar ideas. They were simply not interested in making improvements to a law that they saw as inimical to the satisfactory conduct of industrial relations. This was the clearest possible warning that there would be little "give and take" when the bill reached Parliament in early 1971.

The only occasion I can recall when there was some dialogue with the opposition was when John Prescott (newly elected MP for one of the Hull constituencies, who had previously been an official of the National Union of Seamen) came to see me to warn of the dire consequences of any legislation outlawing the closed shop (where a seaman was required to belong to the NUS). He told me that there was a risk that a seaman who sought to exercise a right not to join the Union would be tipped overboard by his shipmates!

The Parliamentary passage of the Industrial Relations Bill through the House of Commons was contested every inch of the way by Labour MPs, who were particularly incensed by the provisions on trade union membership (and non-membership!). Such was the concentrated fire on these clauses that other sections of the Bill were scarcely examined. Moreover, Labour MPs insisted that the Committee stage of the Bill be taken in the whole House rather than in Committee: thereby precluding much other government business from being discussed.

The Government business managers in the Commons (the Leader of the House and the Chief Whip) were eventually driven to insist on a "Guillotine motion" that would introduce a timetable for debate of the various sections of the Bill. This motion alone took a full day's debate in the Commons! Even with this procedure, however, the Government had to rely largely on the House of Lords to consider and approve a large number of amendments which it wished to make to the legislation, and which the Labour opposition tactics allowed no opportunity to debate.

After spending many uncomfortable and wearisome hours in the official box of the House of Commons over a succession of late night sittings, I was profoundly grateful for the relatively polite and orderly sessions in the Lords . These "rescued" the Bill from the deadlock in the Commons .

My fondest memory of the House of Lords debates was the occasion that Lord Olivier rose to his feet - for the first and only time in the Lords - to argue that the Bill should exclude acting and actors from the closed shop clauses: so that Equity, the actors' trade union, should be able to maintain the requirement that all actors must hold an Equity card before they could appear on the stage. Such a requirement was, in Olivier's view, essential to prevent any Tom ,Dick or Harry seeking to pursue an acting career and driving down the wages of serious professional actors. It was not Olivier's most exciting performance; but we did introduce an amendment which was designed to meet his point (and, incidentally, John Prescott's!).

******

The Industrial Relations Bill completed its Parliamentary passage by the summer recess; and received Royal Assent just as I was departing for our holiday in Dalarna. Never was a holiday more welcome! The Act, as it now became, embodied in large measure the provisions that the original draft Bill had contained - with some amendment to modify the closed shop clauses to meet the problems foreseen by Equity and the National Union of Seamen. Mr Peter Pain, a senior barrister who often crossed swords with Geoffrey Howe when representing employees or unions in court cases, wrote a polite note to Geoffrey complimenting the Government on the drafting of the legislation - but questioning its wisdom! We would soon realise what Pain meant.

Over the following two years, while I remained in the Industrial Relations Division with a responsibility to explain and defend the legislation, the TUC did all in its power to resist or undermine key parts of the Act. In particular it campaigned against the Government's attempts to persuade unions to register in order to secure the benefits of protection against legal sanctions. The TUC did all they could to discourage unions from having anything to do with the newly created National Industrial Relations Court (NIRC) or the Registrar of Trade Unions.

Two events conspired to reinforce the TUC's efforts to destroy the credibility of the Government and the NIRC. The first of these was in July 1972 when five shop stewards were jailed by the NIRC for refusing to obey the Court's order to stop picketing a container depot in East London. Following the arrest and imprisonment of the "Pentonville Five" as they became known, a rolling series of strikes in sympathy with the Five brought about virtually a national unofficial strike. After frantic exchanges between the Government and the President of the Court, a solution to this episode was secured by the Official Solicitor appealing to the Appeal Court against the jailing of the Five by the NIRC. The appeal was allowed, and the Five were released - to the relief of the NIRC and the Government! But the outcome showed how small incidents of challenge to the law, and to the NIRC, could be used to inflame opinion within the trade union movement, and make the government look ridiculous.

Much more serious for the Government was the calling of a national work to rule, and subsequently strike, by the National Union of Mineworkers in 1973. This action was in pursuance of their claim for a pay increase that was contrary to the pay pause that the government had introduced. The NUM had the full support of the TUC, and the trade union movement, in taking strike action. Its picketing activity was successful in depriving many power stations of supplies of coal essential to the running of the electricity grid; and forced the introduction of three-day working in many of Britain's workplaces. The Government was in effect forced to capitulate to the miners' demands; and implicitly to acknowledge that recourse to the IR Act was not a wise response to the NUM pickets.

The successful strike action by the NUM, and the cutting off of electricity that left many people brushing their teeth in the dark, were for the Government the worst possible background for the election called by Edward Heath in February 1974 (in the hope that the country would support the government against the miners). The election saw the Tories defeated - albeit by a small margin. The return of a Labour Government under Harold Wilson led very quickly to the repeal of the Industrial Relations Act in the summer of 1974 : the second significant failure of an elected government to gather support for its approach to industrial relations law. By that time, however, I had been posted to another job. I was glad to have no responsibility for the third attempt within five years to introduce legislation to regulate industrial disputes.

******

I cannot end this chapter without recording my, very limited, involvement in the miners' strike of 1984/85 which did much to destroy the coal industry , leave the trade union movement seriously weakened and reinforce the Thatcher government's approach to industrial relations law.

In the course of a two-year secondment to the Department of Energy, I was appointed to head that Department's Electricity Division a few months before the NUM began its strike action in March 1984.

My main responsibility was to ensure that the nationalised electricity industry, and especially the Central Electricity Generating Board, had the resources and capacity to meet the demand for electrical power across the country.

At that time the industry still depended heavily on reliable deliveries of coal to many of its power stations. The NUM was determined to exploit this vulnerability in pursuit of its strategy to resist the closure of inefficient and uneconomic collieries by the National Coal Board.

The scene was set for a showdown when word got out about the National Coal Board's plan to close down a couple of collieries in the Yorkshire division of the NUM. The strike got under way with a walkout by miners at the Cortonwood Colliery in March 1984.

This time the government was better prepared. It foresaw the NUM strategy, and ensured that the Generating Board had the resources to build up substantial stocks of coal in the months before the coal miners' strike began. It had also ensured that police forces across the country were better coordinated to deal with the threat of mass picketing of collieries and power stations. The government's plans were greatly assisted by two fateful decisions of the NUM and its General Secretary, Arthur Scargill.

First, the calling of the strike in early spring, when demand for power was declining from its winter peak, weakened the leverage of the strikers. More importantly, the NUM refused to carry out a national ballot to secure support for strike action; and in a number of areas - particularly in the Midlands and Lancashire - the miners refused to be dictated to by Scargill and continued to work.

Despite the deployment across the country by the NUM of "flying pickets" and major confrontations between strikers and the police in critical places, supply of electrical power was not seriously threatened. Moreover, the TUC and a number of key unions declined to support the miners; and the general population, though often sympathetic to the miners' cause, had little enthusiasm for Scargill's tactics or aggressive socialist rhetoric. After a year of dwindling morale and falling public support, and recognition that the government was not to be swayed from its determination to close uneconomic pits, the NUM called off its industrial action in March 1985.

It was, in many respects, the end of an era . The years of the pre-eminence of the miners within the union movement were effectively ended - and many mining communities were destroyed by the programme of colliery closures that followed the end of the strike. More generally, the impact of the legislation introduced by the

Thatcher government in the 1980s to require a ballot before strike action called for major modifications to trade union tactics in pursuing their objectives. Moreover the influence of the TUC and the union movement on key government policies was much weakened.

For me, it was my last engagement in government efforts to construct an acceptable legal framework that would operate "in place of strife".

OFFICE OF HOPE**

After four years devoted to the tangled policies of industrial relations, I was posted in early 1973 to the ESA, where I was to assume the duties of Director of Planning in the newly created Agency. It was an area of Government business where I had no previous experience; and which would make very different demands - managerial, financial, operational and technological - from those I experienced in shaping policy on industrial relations. But I was delighted to engage in yet another of the Department's "problem areas" after my experience with industrial training and industrial relations.

As I hinted in an earlier chapter, there was much concern among senior officials in the Ministry of Labour when I entered the Department at the decline in the authority and impact of the public employment service during the post war period. Successive Ministers of Labour had not attached much importance to the effectiveness of the Employment Exchanges: either because they regarded industrial relations as their main priority, or because they remained in their posts too short a time to get a grip on the Ministry's key function of supporting the efficient operation of the labour market. The Employment Exchanges had a "dole queue image" among both employers and jobseekers; and were seen by their "customers" as

**Footnote: The title of this Chapter is taken from the title of "A History of the Employment Service" by David Price, published in 2005 by the Policy Studies Institute. This is a deeply researched , authoritative and balanced study of the vicissitudes of the Employment Service from its foundation in 1910 to the end of the twentieth century. David Price was a close colleague of mine throughout my time as Director of Planning and then Chief Executive of the Employment Service Agency (the ESA, as it was known in the mid-1970s); and he remained with the service as Deputy Chief Executive for some years after my departure. Nobody is better placed to assess the changes wrought in the service over the past century. I acknowledge the help his volume has given me in recalling important details of my time with the Employment Service Agency (ESA) .

bureaucratic in appearance and approach. Though the Exchanges were efficient in ensuring that the unemployed were promptly and correctly paid their benefit, this essential function seemed to dominate the work of finding and filling job vacancies. Moreover, the Treasury often saw the staffing levels in the Exchanges as suitable points of attack in the Government's efforts to rein in public expenditure; and the Ministry was not adept at fending off the Treasury. This had the inevitable effect that the employment service was something of a Cinderella in the allocation of staff resources to vacancy filling.

The 1960s saw the beginnings of an important sea-change. Within the Department, this was driven by Sir James Dunnett, (always known as Ned) who was appointed Permanent Secretary in 1962. Dunnett appeared, on first acquaintance, a rather dour and private individual, who often left one uncertain about his views. But he had a keen sense of what was important. After a spell as Permanent Secretary at the Department of Transport driving forward a major programme of investment in motorways, he had a sure grip on what was needed to manage a large government programme. He quickly saw that a strong initiative was needed to modernise the employment service. He was egged on by some of his senior officials, who had for some time been waiting for opportunity and encouragement to voice their ideas for a more activist employment service.

Dunnett set up a Working Party, under his chairmanship, to examine what changes were needed to invigorate the employment service and give it a clearer vision of its role in the operation of the labour market in an increasingly competitive world. The report of this Working Party marked the start of a process of reform which would, over the following decade, revolutionise the operations and ambitions of the service.

There were also external pressures for change. Within the Government, attempts to stimulate economic growth were seen to call for a more positive approach to labour market problems. And, internationally, the importance of "positive labour market policies" was stressed by the Organisation for Economic Development and Cooperation (OECD). Furthermore, the report of the Fulton Committee on the Civil Service (in 1968) emphasized the need to give much more attention to improving the management of government services. This message was seized on by officials in the Department to gain greater leverage with the Treasury and to urge stronger support from Ministers for modernising the employment service.

The key features of the modernisation programme, as it developed from a range of official studies and operational experiments in the sixties to the ambitious strategy agreed by the Heath Government in the early seventies, can be summarised as follows:

--the separation of employment work from the Ministry of Labour's benefit payment functions, and the introduction of a management structure geared exclusively to improving the operation of the labour market and gaining greater credibility with jobseekers and employers;

--a major improvement in the attractiveness, location and visibility of employment offices, leading to the establishment of a national network of Jobcentres ,sited wherever possible in the main shopping centres;

-the introduction of Self Service displays in Jobcentres to enable vacancies to be more visible and to help jobseekers to choose for themselves the jobs they would like to be offered;

-raising the calibre, and improving the training, of employment advisors, so that the key staff in Jobcentres were better equipped to offer authoritative advice and guidance to jobseekers and employers ;

-the introduction of Occupational Guidance Units in a number of the larger Jobcentres to help , especially, those wishing to change their occupation or widen their career options.

Many of these initiatives were driven forward by officials. But the arrival of Barbara Castle as Secretary of State for Employment had a galvanising effect. She needed little persuading of the importance of modernising the employment service; and she gave officials the support they needed, in particular, to overcome the hesitations of the Department of Social Security about the separation of employment and benefit payment functions. Indeed, at a critical moment in the debate about separation, Barbara Castle had a blazing row with her colleague and friend, Richard Crossman, Secretary of State for Social Security, about the merits of separating the management of the benefit payment and employment service functions of the Department of Employment. Prime Minister Harold Wilson was forced to intervene. The upshot was that Barbara won the argument; and for the following decade or more separation became the accepted Government stance.

Even more significant was the commitment of the Heath Government, and Robert Carr, the Employment Secretary, to the modernisation strategy. Carr was attracted to the idea of setting up the employment service as one of the Executive Agencies to be established as (more or less) self governing enterprises within the government service to deliver major programmes. These Agencies were to operate at arm's length from their parent Department, and have their own management team and budget. Thus it was that the employment service became the Employment Service Agency; and Ken Cooper was appointed its first Chief Executive.

Ken was an unusually forceful, charismatic and visionary civil servant. He had been brought up in a family of officers in the Salvation Army, and was familiar with the crusading character of the Army. That stood him in good stead in leading the ESA's campaign to establish itself as a marketing force. He was helped by the considerable degree of independence from Ministers and the Department which the ESA enjoyed when it became an arm of the Manpower Services Commission (MSC): the independent tripartite body the Government decided to set up in 1973/4 to supervise the Training Services and Employment Services Agencies of the Department.

By the end of 1972, Ken Cooper and his team were able to put to Ministers an Action Programme, which provided for the ESA to assume responsibility for the public employment service, shorn of benefit payment functions, with its own management and a new regional structure of 18 Areas. The Plan outlined a programme to establish 400 jobcentres over a 7 year period; and put a new emphasis on marketing the service to employers. This Action Programme was published at the end of 1972; and became the basis for the most radical overhaul of the service since its foundation in 1910.

It was shortly after the publication of the Action Programme that I joined the ESA to become its Planning Director (though for some months I also had a general oversight of policy on the operation of the employment service). Much of the role and future of the ESA had been settled. What could or should I contribute?

In my early months, I gave a great deal of thought to what was required to establish a satisfactory basis for operational planning, financial accounting and performance management. I talked over with officials from the Civil Service Department ideas which they had been considering, in the wake of the Fulton Report, to ensure better performance and accountability in Government Agencies. I also imbibed a number of the lessons drawn by management consultants about managing performance in the public sector. I began to appreciate the vital importance of a computerised management information and financial accounting system to decision taking within the ESA.

With this in mind, I commissioned a team of management consultants from Coopers and Lybrand to advise on how the ESA might best establish the necessary systems; and I set up under my chairmanship an Accountability Steering Committee to supervise the work of the consultants and to advise the ESA management team on the recommendations emerging from the Coopers study.

By December 1974, Coopers had produced a massive report on a new management information system. This was viewed with some alarm by some of my senior colleagues, who feared that we might be strangled by an unduly complex management information structure. However, the Coopers report paved the way for a computerised Financial and Management Accounting System (FMAS), which distinguished the important programmes and sub programmes whose outputs and resources would be the critical elements for the purposes of planning and managerial decision-making. This became in some respects a model for accountable management within other Government Agencies. More importantly, it provided the base for the development of the ESA's Operational Planning System which would set out, year by year, the Agency's priorities, the resources which could be committed to the priorities, and the plans and targets for each Area. By the time I was appointed to succeed Ken Cooper as Chief Executive, some of the benefits of this "groundwork" were evident in the decision making of the ESA's Executive Committee and the setting of plans and targets at Area level.

In May 1973 there landed on my desk a report by Bruce Graham of PA Management Consultants , recommending a comprehensive real-time computer scheme for supporting the placing work of the employment service in the London area. This was the starting point for my 6-year involvement in, and promotion of, what became known as the CAPITAL Project (the acronym I suggested for Computer Assisted Placing in the Areas of London).

The London labour market was so vast and complex that the relatively simple clerical processes that might serve a modest-sized town were inadequate for handling the wide range of vacancy and jobseeker information in London. PA had therefore been commissioned by the Department and Ken Cooper's team to explore options for computerising the handling of manpower data and the matching of vacancies and jobseekers. The PA report recommended a pilot scheme in a sector of North East London which would give Jobcentres instant access to notified vacancies and registered jobseekers throughout this part of London, and the capacity to identify potential matches and rapidly submit jobseekers to employers. PA envisaged that the computer system would be supplied by a mainframe manufacturer as a bureau service - so that, if the experiment was unsuccessful, the ESA would not be left with computers and a large number of VDUs that were not required on a long term basis.

The PA report was an exceptionally ambitious document, which envisaged the ESA attempting a groundbreaking experiment without any precedent elsewhere in the world. It would move the London service from reliance on a simple fax system for circulating information about notified vacancies (which was widely recognised as inadequate) to a computer-based operation where every vacancy was instantly accessible on VDUs and self-service notice boards in every employment office. And this information was to be paralleled by corresponding information on jobseekers. Could we take the risk of such a major operational change at one leap?

I had no significant experience of computerisation of government operations; and I found it difficult to assess the problems that would have to be confronted. But I judged that the proposed pilot scheme would be the right path to follow; and that the risk of disaster should not deter us from recognising the potential benefits of success. Several meetings with senior officials in the Government's Central Computer Agency persuaded Ken Cooper and me that the pilot project was worth pursuing. The ESA Executive Committee was of similar mind. We decided to secure the backing of the Department and the Treasury for the investment; and when that was forthcoming we decided to take the plunge; and set up the pilot in 15 employment offices in a depressed area of North East London.

Two problems concerned me as I considered the best way of getting the project established. First, there were some signs that the ESA's London management were hesitant or unconvinced about the importance of the project. It would be essential for senior people from the ESA in London to be fully engaged in the team to manage the project. Second, I was unhappy about the capacity of the provisional team leader to give the project the drive and authority required. On the first problem, I insisted that a senior representative of the London Director was fully involved in the Steering Committee I was to chair; and that there was an employment office manager on the implementation team. On the second problem, I was fortunate to be able to recruit from the CCA a very able Principal with wide experience of Government computing who had been involved in the PA study. Brian White came over to the ESA, on promotion to Senior Principal, to take command of the project team. It was the best decision I took in my time as Director of Planning

A third key decision was the company to provide the Mainframe computer bureau services: Honeywell got the nod, after I had seen an indication of their quality during a visit to Sweden at the end of 1973.

In the build up to live operation during 1974 and 1975, Brian White's project management team proved very effective in gaining the wholehearted engagement of the ESA London managers and staff. With the support of PA and Honeywell, the technical problems were also tackled with considerable success. The only major hiccup was the opposition of the trade unions to one aspect of the computerisation. That concerned the categorisation of some unemployed jobseekers as having limited skill or suitable employment record. The Civil and Public Services Association, representing the clerical staff, saw this as harming the prospects of jobseekers who needed and deserved special help from the ESA. When I became Chief Executive in early 1976, this dispute showed signs of blocking all progress on the project. My Deputy gave an effective presentation to the Manpower Services Commission explaining why it was necessary to include in jobseeker profiles information about eg recent employment record and skills. The Commission endorsed our general approach; but encouraged me to seek a reconciliation with the trade unions. As I recall, we were able to tweak the system sufficiently to satisfy the CPSA that we had no intention of "blacking" groups of jobseekers. The threat of industrial action was withdrawn; but it was a warning sign of the disquiet that existed within the ranks of the clerical staff about computerisation (and of the militant posture of some trade unions at this time).

After intensive efforts, the pilot scheme went live in 1977 in a somewhat depressed area of North East London. The switchover to the new system went remarkably smoothly, both technically and operationally. Soon there was interest from many parts of the world in what was, in many respects, a groundbreaking approach: especially in using computer terminals to identify suitable matches . The Deputy Prime Minister of Sweden was perhaps the most notable overseas visitor; and following up his interest, I conducted in the summer of 1977 a seminar at the Swedish Labour Market Board in Stockholm on the way the ESA had shaped the project. What was also very gratifying was that, in 1978, the CAPITAL project won the British Computer Society's award for the most successful application of computers to a Government service.

The key questions about cost effectiveness, however, remained to be answered.

There was great pressure to evaluate the experiment, both from the Department and Manpower Services Commission. We were bound to assess the project financially according to strict guidelines set by the Treasury (which in this case depended heavily on the speed of placings- a key indicator of the cost/benefit and the efficiency of computerisation). David Price was largely responsible for producing an evaluation report as early as July 1978, based on only a few months of experience. This evaluation estimated that CAPITAL increased placings by 10% and reduced vacancy duration by around 20% (or about half a day). On this evidence, I sought the agreement of the MSC to extending the Project to the whole of London, at an estimated cost of £11 million. The top management of the Commission and Commissioners themselves supported the extension. But by late 1978 we ran into difficulties with the trade unions, which held up progress and - as it turned out - delayed a final decision to proceed until mid 1979 - by which time a Conservative Government, determined to bring down public expenditure, had won a general election,(and I had been posted to head the MSC's Training Services Division!)

Whilst the project could happily survive my departure, the combination of trade union opposition, substantial manpower cuts in ESA staffing and growing doubts in the ESA's management about continuing the project in a climate of staffing cuts led the ESA Executive to the conclusion that CAPITAL should be replaced by a much less ambitious Vacancy circulation system. My protestations on the MSC's senior management committee that this course would be a dreadful waste of the experience and success of CAPITAL fell on deaf ears. To this day I have nurtured a sense of a lost opportunity! In the event, the proposed vacancy system did not go live for another 8 years, which only added salt to my wounds!

******

As I have already mentioned, I was appointed Chief Executive of the ESA in the early months of 1976, when John Cassels was promoted to a new post of Director of the MSC, and Ken Cooper replaced him as Chief Executive of the Training Services Division. My appointment occasioned a little political "drama".

When the Commission Chairman, Sir Richard O'Brien, proposed my appointment there was opposition from the trade union members. They felt, presumably, that consideration should be given to people outside the civil service; and that the Commission itself should take

the decision rather than have an internal candidate "imposed" on them. I learned of this from the Department's Permanent Secretary, Sir Conrad Heron. He sought my views about a response to this development. I made it clear that I would not be willing to accept the appointment if a number of MSC members---albeit a minority
- had serious reservations about me. When this was fed back to the Commission at its next meeting. the trade union group withdrew their objections, and accepted, with good grace, that a majority of the Commission had agreed on my appointment and they accepted that decision. They suggested however that I should be interviewed by three Commissioners before my appointment was confirmed.

When interviewed by the three Commission members, I was of course questioned about my views on the ESA's priorities. I emphasized that I was fully committed to the proposals in the 1974 submission "Plans and Programmes" (much of which I had drafted), but I judged that the Agency should do more to help jobseekers at the margins of the labour market: either because of lengthy periods of unemployment or loss of confidence and motivation. I hoped that the success and effectiveness of the newly established Jobcentres would release the resources to provide the extra help and support for jobseekers with special needs. This would be one of the themes of my three years as Chief Executive.

My first steps as Chief Executive were to reassure managers and staff that I was 100 per cent committed to the modernisation programme approved by the Commission in 1974. I hoped that there would be a period of steady consolidation without serious challenges to the ESA's objectives of increased penetration of the job market. I also promised to spend at least one day a week visiting Jobcentres and Area Offices to understand better some of the problems local managers faced in improving the service they offered.

I also sought to combine this "steady as you go" promise with particular attention to several new developments.

The first of these was to sharpen our approach to performance management by some form of "Management by Objectives": under which managers at every level committed to goals for which they would be held accountable. Some of my steps in this direction attracted a good deal of scepticism; but the operational planning system introduced in 1974/5 served as a reasonably rigorous starting point for the setting of clearly defined and precise objectives at every level of management.

My second concern, mentioned above, was to move towards a scheme that provided for extra support for unemployed jobseekers whom it was difficult to ease into satisfactory jobs. After a great deal of discussion we eventually developed a Special Employment Needs programme, under which employment advisors identified individuals with significant problems and worked through various possibilities for helping them to become more "jobready". By the time I left the ESA, the impact of this scheme was positive but limited in extent - and rising unemployment in the late 1970s made substantial progress much more difficult.

Thirdly, I remained very committed to the experiments in computerisation flowing from the Coopers and PA reports - and in particular to the CAPITALand the Financial and Management Accounting System (FMAS). In operational and technical terms both these projects proved successful; but as I have explained above the benefits of CAPITAL were sacrificed following the cuts made by the Thatcher government.

The sharp rise in unemployment in the later 1970s presented the Employment Service Division (ESD as it became known from 1977) with uncomfortable challenges and choices. In 1974, the unemployed numbered 619000 (2.6% of the working population); by 1979 that figure had more than doubled, to about 1.4 million(around 5.7% of the working population). With this increase came an ever larger number of jobseekers who had been unemployed for

6 months or more. I faced sharp questioning from the Department of Employment and the Department of Social Security on whether the strategic plans agreed in 1974 ("Plans and Programmes"), which placed considerable emphasis on securing a larger share of the labour market and a major investment in new Jobcentres, remained appropriate in the difficult conditions of the late 1980s and early 1990s. Should we not give greater priority to assisting the unemployed - and especially the longer unemployed-- than our business model implied? And should Jobcentre managers not give more attention to ensuring that the unemployed were genuinely looking for jobs and not "shirking"?

My view and that of my senior management team was that the rising levels of unemployment did not necessarily call for a fundamental change of direction. The more successful the ESD was in increasing the numbers of vacancies notified by employers - and the better our credit with employers - the more opportunities we would be able to offer the unemployed. The modernisation of the service, and the increasing number of well situated Jobcentres, should enable the ESD to provide the most efficient service to both employers and the unemployed. I emphasized , therefore, that the priority we were giving to finding and filling the maximum number of job vacancies remained the best way of serving the interests of the unemployed as well as employers (and the national economy). I also pointed out the unhappy experience of the employment service of the USA which, in the 1960s, had concentrated on helping the unemployed, and had suffered a severe fall in the number of placings and loss of credibility.

I nonetheless accepted that some special assistance to those having greater difficulty in getting a foothold in the job market should be a part of our developing approach; and this was the reason why we introduced the Special Employment Needs experiment in 1977. This programme was not specifically addressed to the longer term unemployed. We felt that a more important objective was to prevent jobseekers becoming long term unemployed, by measures directed to assisting unemployed in the early stages of their time on the register.

Whatever the force and logic of these arguments, the concern of the Department of Employment, and indeed of some MSC Commissioners, about the plight of the unemployed led the Chairman and Director of the Commission to propose, in May 1978, a major review of the employment service. This Review was intended to pose some hard questions and reconsider some of the priorities and objectives of the ESD.

John Cassels , the MSC Director, set up and chaired a Steering Group to carry out this review. I did not take a direct part in the review but ensured that ESD senior management was deeply involved; and the ESD provided the Secretariat.

The Steering Group's report was delivered to the Manpower Services Commission in the summer of 1979 . It began with an emphatic endorsement of the achievements of the service since 1974. At least 100 Jobcentres had been opened each year; job filling performance had improved by 25 %; overall; and placings had risen to 1.8 millions, the highest number since 1956 (despite the mounting numbers of unemployed). The cost of placings had proved lower in Jobcentres than in other employment offices; and the evidence also pointed to speedier placings. Well trained employment advisers and self-service facilities had been introduced throughout the local office network. Modernisation had also benefited the long-term unemployed ,since Jobcentres achieved more submissions and placings with the longer unemployed than had other employment offices.

The report acknowledged that there might be a point where deeper penetration by ESD would not be cost effective; but it argued that:" It is above all the share of vacancies which it handles which determines whether the service is able to function effectively." Without this grip on the market, the ESD was not able to fulfil its other roles effectively.

The report's general conclusion was encapsulated in its final paragraph:

"From being a rundown service, often poorly regarded by both employers and jobseekers, the employment service has secured the respect of both and has become a stronger and more positive force in the labour market. Underlying the statistics is the reality of the transformation of the search for work from a depressed backstreet operation to a normal activity conducted in businesslike conditions in which those concerned - employers, jobseekers and employment service staff - have the tools to do the job. The rise in unemployment underlines how timely this transformation has been".

The Manpower Services Commission's endorsement of the Cassels report provided for me, as I moved to take over as Chief Executive of the MSC's Training Services Division, a very positive farewell assessment on my time with the ESD. But I was well aware, from my seat in the MSC Chairman's Management Committee, that the Thatcher government was all too likely to challenge the MSC's judgement, and subject the ESD to a more critical scrutiny. This would call into question many of aspects of the modernisation programme for which I had fought.

REFLECTIONS AT FIFTY

I was posted back to the Department of Employment - my official "home"- at the beginning of 1985, to take up the post of Director of Personnel and Management Services. After nearly a decade with the Manpower Services Commission in three senior positions, I was glad to return to a post which offered a very different challenge.

As I made my way back to the DE, I reflected that my decade with the MSC was much the same period that my young family were going through their teenage years. My recollections of my time with the MSC are, I hope, sufficiently revealed in previous chapters. It is time to turn back to the family.

It's commonly said that the teenage years are the most difficult and challenging, both to the "young persons" themselves and to their parents: both parties need to "grow up" in order to leave behind reasonably happy individuals who will want to retain a strong bond with each other in the "after-life" of mature adulthood they hope to share.

How did Berit (always Mamma to our children) and I manage the growing up?

The truth is that I don't know for sure! At times I am coyly satisfied that we didn't do too badly. We remained a close knit family, who talk to each other often; care about each other; and don't harbour anxieties that any one of the other family members is being specially favoured. But at other times I am critical of the way I dealt with the problems that any family must confront: I feel that I threw too much responsibility on to Berit; that I was too often an absentee dad; that I didn't engage sufficiently with the children when they needed me; and that I was often a poor communicator, unwilling to face up to difficult situations . I hope this account will avoid both the tragic and the complacent judgement - which is probably about right?

The title of the second part of this Memoir is "A Partnership". Berit and I entered into marriage determined that neither of us would be boss. Even if we couldn't share responsibilities equally in all circumstances, we would be sure that on all important occasions the judgments we made would be shared. In all its ups and downs, I think that Berit and I - Mamma and Pappa - generally maintained a genuine partnership: of love and trust, honesty and consistency; sharing in all important decisions. This was sustained, I have to confess, in large part by Berit's warmth; her ingrained sense of fairness; her ability to say the harsh things when they needed to be said; and by her humanity and insight. And above all by her love: not many days went by without her repeating, to me or our children, "I love you"! I think our children were reassured by our relationship of love and trust, and appreciated the fact that we tried very hard to support one another consistently. I also hope that they had some fun!

I believe that our partnership was both tested and then strengthened in the late 1970s by Berit's taking up part-time employment with Surrey County Council's Waverley Social Services team. Although she got some satisfaction from the experiences she had in voluntary work as a counsellor in matrimonial disputes and recovery from grief, she had always looked forward to using her skills and training as a social worker when domestic commitments and caring responsibilities became less pressing. When Karin reached secondary school, Berit felt that the time was ripe to explore the possibility of employment. Surrey Social Services were very ready to take her on; and rapidly assigned her to a small team working on support and guidance for vulnerable clients of all ages.

Although her section head was not the most supportive or considerate boss, Berit adjusted quickly to the new challenges and formed excellent working relationships with her immediate colleagues. She faced a range of problems in supporting clients, often with very restricted financial resources. But the work provided rewards she could not expect as a mother: notably a network of new friends and colleagues and the satisfaction of giving her clients an improved ability and confidence in coming to grips with their problems and claiming any financial support they were entitled to.(Berit herself had no special financial package to offer them).

I believe it helped our children to realise that they must accept greater responsibility for their behaviour and decisions - and encouraged them in other ways to become less dependent. And there's no doubt that , with Berit developing a new role outside the home, our children too began to "spread their wings" and become more active beyond the home (sometimes in ways of which Berit and I would be unaware!).

******

Another challenge to the family in this period was my move to Sheffield in1982 to join up with the rest of the Headquarters staff of my Training Division team, whose posts were being relocated to Sheffield as part of the Government's programme of devolving significant services to the provinces. The MSC was in the vanguard of this programme of devolution, partly because , as a semi-independent organisation, it was not judged essential to be based in London. Though this move was unquestionably a great boon to the Sheffield community in its darkest post-war hour, it meant considerable inconvenience to many London based MSC staff. I judged it essential therefore that I lead the move of my Division, even though I anticipated that my future postings would probably be back in London, and that I could not expect my stay in Sheffield to be permanent. For that reason there was no question of moving house and family. I therefore took up temporary rented accommodation close to the newly erected Moorfoot Headquarters that the MSC had acquired in the centre of Sheffield.

I cannot say that my year in Sheffield was a happy experience - though I was glad to work alongside my colleagues in the Division, and found satisfaction in discovering something of the character and spirit of

Sheffield and South Yorkshire. I would spend the week in Sheffield, or travelling up and down between Sheffield and London; then return to Godalming to be home for the weekends. It was an exhausting regime. I pined for contact with the family; and I was concerned at the extra burden placed on both Berit and our children. I would get home late on Fridays and have to set off for Sheffield early on Mondays; and found it difficult to get stuck in to family "business" to a satisfactory extent during the weekends. It created inevitable strains on all of us. I had to look to Andrew during the week to help look after our newly acquired German Shepherd, Tosca; and hope that other essential family duties could be deferred to the weekends.

I was fortunate that the offer of a two year secondment to the Department of Energy in London came my way after of year of this weekly commuting regime. I departed both the MSC and Sheffield in early 1983, with some relief; and with a feeling that neither my career nor my family life had benefited from this experience of temporary relocation. (I should add, however, that the move of this large body of Government servants to Sheffield was widely regarded , even among most of those who were forced to move permanently, to be a significant success. The functions remain to this day mainly based in Sheffield; and the introduction of video-conference facilities and email has of course made communication between Sheffield and London a great deal easier and more efficient).

******

When I consider how our family's way of life developed during these "adolescent years", I naturally think first how each of our children experienced the challenges they faced as they moved towards their A Level exams and the life beyond. This is what I wish to discuss in the concluding sections of this Memoir.

Nick (as Nicholas became from his early years at Godalming College) comes first into view. The characteristic which we all recognised in

Nick was his intense and effective focus on the tasks he set himself, whether as a pupil, a musician, a sportsman or as a traveller. I can recall Nick, in his early days, climbing up our elm trees as though he looked to life as a monkey. And , later on , he was determined to show the rest of the family how to walk on stilts up and down the driveway, long after we had given up the attempt to master the skill. Later still, he spent much time exercising with his "Bullworker" to improve his physical strength. He was conscious he was , physically, a late developer and he needed to prove himself as fit and active as any of his peers.

Most importantly, throughout his schooldays, Nick was always an extremely dedicated and diligent pupil: he enjoyed both the challenge and the success he experienced in a wide range of subjects. He was as much at home in languages and history as in maths and the sciences. He was almost always near the top of the class; and made no bones about the fact that he enjoyed being so. He showed the same determination in his progress through the exam stages in playing the piano, which he reckoned even more testing than school exams.

Nick was, from his early teens, always clear that he was going to pursue a career in medicine (perhaps influenced by the fact that Berit's two brothers were doctors). This choice led to a decision to settle on physics, chemistry and biology as his A level targets. His progress towards the necessary grades for entry to medical school was cruelly threatened when , in his final year, he contracted an unusually severe bout of glandular fever. This left him very exhausted just at the time he was in the final stages of preparation for his A level exams. He was, moreover, not helped by his struggles with the symptoms of anorexia. He refused to contemplate deferring his exams, and struggled manfully on towards his goal of a place at the Leicester University Medical School. In the event, he achieved the necessary grades - though I believe that the effects of the fever meant that he did not reach the levels he merited. This outcome was a tribute to Nick's single-minded determination - and a great relief, as well as pride, for Berit and me.

It would be wrong of me to imply that academic achievement was the be-all and end-all of Nick's life. He was very much an all- rounder. He adored music: whether struggling over a Beethoven sonata towards the grade 7 exam; or relaxing with his uncle Jan as they listened together to the Beatles' Sergeant Pepper whilst he was on holiday in Sweden. He even claimed to enjoy the Sex pistols! Playing or listening, music would always be a key part of his future way of life.

I have also happy memories of striding with Nick - often with our dog Tosca - over the sandy hills of Puttenham Common on our weekend work outs. We agreed that this circuit of three steep climbs was the acid test of our credentials. And for a year or so we also took part in the occasional orienteering competition: though Nick was so much fitter, and so much more reliable a navigator, that he had no difficulty leaving me far behind!

Besides cross-country running Nick also took football seriously: especially as a supporter of Leeds United (He claimed that his loyalty to Leeds and their Manager ceased when the club made what he regarded as a "fiscal Faustian pact" with the Premier League authorities). A keen interest in, and considerable knowledge of, the game would remain with him into the future.

Nick left home in the Autumn of 1979 to embark on a "Gap Year" which would start with some weeks of travel across Europe, to be followed by several months as, in essence, a care assistant in a home for disadvantaged children. This combination of travel and care for others would be important commitments of his life.

At the end of Nick's gap year the whole family gathered for a summer holiday in the south of Sweden . It was a singularly happy time. Nick was looking forward eagerly to the start of his medical course at Leicester; and we enjoyed a stay in an area we had not previously explored . (As things turned out, it was to be the last Swedish holiday we spent together as a family . It also proved to be the start of our children's passage to adulthood.

******

With Nick's departure to Leicester, Andrew became the "senior sibling" in the household.

The characteristic that we regarded as most notable in Andrew was his independent-mindedness. Berit and I saw evidence of this quality as early as Andrew's first term at Shackleford Primary School. At the School's Christmas Carol service, he contradicted his teacher's instructions and insisted that his class process to their appointed station in the Church by a different route from that prescribed. He would not be denied; and his teacher accepted with good grace that the kids would go where Andrew pointed!

Move on eight years, and Andrew is nearing the end of his time at Haslemere Preparatory School, where he has been very much at home as a pupil and a star miler. He has just passed his Common Entrance Exam, preparatory to moving on to public school in the autumn of 1977.

Berit and I had for some time been planning to enrol Andrew at Charterhouse, a school conveniently located less than a mile from Groton . The school had recently begun to take boys as day pupils, which we had always regarded as important. In discussion with the Headmaster, Oliver Van Oss, we learned that Andrew would be welcome at Charterhouse. We also gathered that the school under Van Oss had a somewhat less authoritarian regime than some public schools at that time. Caning was gone; and the school welcomed contacts with parents as a sensible means of resolving problems pupils might face in adapting to academic and other challenges. We felt that Andrew should be happy at Charterhouse; and any qualms we might have had were settled by our meeting with his prospective housemaster, John Phillips, who struck us as genial and approachable.

Andrew was therefore enrolled at Charterhouse in September 1977,as a dayboy, but with a place in Gownboys, one of the original boarding houses. Here he would mix with the boarders and spend much of his out-of-class hours. He would expect to return home in the evenings to be with the family, and do his homework. We hoped that this would get the best of both worlds: genuine integration into the life of Charterhouse combined with continuing contact with his family. How did it work out?

Although Andrew settled reasonably smoothly into his new life, and seldom complained about the challenges it presented, Berit and I felt increasingly over the next few years that Andrew did not thrive as Nick had done at Godalming College. It was difficult to pin down the reasons for this. He did not have many close friends among fellow Carthusians: indeed his closest friend was Andrew Stokes, who was a student at Guildford Grammar School. He did not excel at, or indeed much enjoy, the team games - football, hockey and cricket - that were the core of Charterhouse's non-academic life: Andrew's main sporting strengths were in cross-country running, a more solitary sport. In the classroom, he was an average performer with no marked enthusiasms or achievements to elicit encouragement from the "Beaks" - and he occasionally was very critical about the quality of his teachers.

Underlying all this, we sometimes felt that, fundamentally, Andrew did not "buy in" to the Charterhouse ethos. He would have been happier with a regime that was less socially elitist, and more open to sharp questions and direct challenge. But he seldom aired his criticisms with us: perhaps mindful of the significant financial investment we had made in his education.

However, he soldiered on conscientiously through to his GCSEs .His results prompted some questions from his teachers about whether he would benefit from progression to the Sixth Form. This spurred his determination to prove his mettle! With a shift to subjects he was more comfortable with, and to teachers he respected, he increased substantially his academic focus . This paid off. In the A level exams in the summer of 1982, he removed doubts about his potential with a set of results which met the requirements for entry into the English department of York University. I recall very clearly driving Andrew to Charterhouse to learn how he had done - and the shy grin that showed me his delight that he had really achieved something, for us as well as himself!

One of the advantages Andrew enjoyed as a dayboy at Charterhouse was the opportunity this gave him to disengage from the close supervision of the "Beaks" and get away to activities of his choosing. This chimed with his independent spirit. We often did not know what he chose to do with himself; or where he got to on his bicycle or out with his friends. But one particular project of his did become known to us; and became sufficient of a "cause-celebre" to merit a mention in this Memoir.

As a result of contacts with a school friend whose family owned a farm and, among other things, bred ferrets, Andrew found himself the possessor of a pair of ferrets. He had evidently discussed with his close friend, Andrew Stokes, a plan to train these animals to hunt rabbits; and between hunting expeditions the animals would be domiciled in hutches in the Browns' and Stokes's gardens. This much we were told only when the ferrets had already arrived!

I don't recall how often these rabbiting expeditions took place; or whether the boys had any success. I certainly don't remember having any rabbit pie! I do remember, however, that Andrew took his ferret back to her birthplace one weekend to "associate conjugally" with a suitable male. I also remember the arrival of several baby ferrets! We insisted that Andrew return these arrivals to the farm where they were conceived. He clearly could not undertake to be responsible for looking after, feeding and protecting, the whole family.

Later on, and more seriously, Andrew's ferret managed to escape from her hutch in our garden, and make her way to another garden, where she took her revenge on a chicken owned by one of the Charterhouse masters. Embarrassed apologies all round! There could be no question of retaining in our garden a ferret which could not be properly controlled. So back to her birthplace the unfortunate creature was returned. And further rabbiting would be left to a family who had sufficient expertise to manage ferrets!

I would like to think that this experience of animal husbandry might have been of some value to Andrew as he ,shortly after his A level exams, embarked on a gap year focused on experience on a kibbutz in Israel followed by a spell on a dairy farm in France. But I suspect that in neither case would ferrets have been a part of his responsibilities.

******

Two key events shaped and inspired Karin's teenage years.

The first was her acquisition, as a twelfth birthday present, of a part-share in a New Forest pony called Brandy. The second was her enrolment in Godalming Sixth Form College, as a sixteen year old, in September 1982.

From an early age, Karin enjoyed being with horses. I recall her having her first riding lessons as an eight year old, and developing an enthusiasm both for the physical activity of riding and the activities associated with horses: schooling, caring, mucking out and, of course, the social contacts and friendships that grew out of her regular outings. Over the years this enthusiasm grew into a passion; and Berit and I became persuaded that Karin should have her own horse, so that she could become a more competent and disciplined rider.

We discovered another family looking for a horse for their daughter, Katy; and we decided to take a part share with them in a relatively young New Forest pony. We hoped this would be a suitable introduction to the responsibilities and opportunities of ownership. Brandy seemed to Berit an amenable animal, and not too challenging; I judged him an attractive brown colour. So the die was cast; and Brandy joined the family and was stabled at a farm in Compton. This would quickly become almost a second home for Karin over the following three years; and certainly the main focus for her leisure activities. As it turned out, Karin had the overwhelming share of riding Brandy, because her friend Katy did not develop the same passion for riding and soon became something of an absentee owner.

By the time Karin was sixteen, and had a good deal of experience and skill as a rider (including participation in gymkhanas and shows etc), the opportunity came for her to acquire on temporary loan a bigger and more challenging horse whilst his owner was out of the country. Karin jumped at this chance; and March now became her main ride until the imminence of A Level exams forced a halt (and the sale of Brandy, and the return of March to his owner).

Looking back over these (nearly) five years, it is clear to me that this experience of, and passion for , horses and horsemanship, gave Karin a highly attractive alternative life away from school and family. It enabled her to find herself a pastime that she found fulfilling in several different ways: a physical challenge; a group of close friends among her fellow riders; a growing understanding of horses and how to handle them; and a satisfying level of skill and confidence as a rider. It was also very satisfying for Berit that her daughter would get the same enjoyment from riding as she (Berit) had had as a teenager growing up in Stockholm. Seldom has the purchase of a birthday present proved more rewarding!

By the time Karin had taken her GCSE exams at her private girls' school, Tormead, she had wearied of the somewhat cosseted and restrictive atmosphere the school offered. She was ready for the more adult and robust culture of Godalming College; and it is there she enrolled for the autumn term of 1982. (She would have wished to follow Andrew to Charterhouse, but we judged that the intense competition would almost certainly have denied her a place)

She found the College , in her estimation, "fabulous" and "a wonderful social platform". With her notable gift for friendship she soon gathered about her a wide circle of friends (of both sexes). And because she was always a good listener, with an empathetic insight into others' situations, she attracted loyal friends who valued her company and advice. Therefore the "social whirl" absorbed a good deal of her time and energy(when she was not riding!).

As she would be the first to admit, the academic side of her Sixth Form experience suffered. Her devotion to the English and French syllabuses was fitful; and not stimulated by the quality of the teaching or the rigour of supervision. The French teacher, in particular, was a disaster. Though Karin was more stimulated by the content and teaching of Media Studies, that was not enough to secure her respectable results in her A Level exams in English and French. She faced the harsh reality that, if she wanted to get a place at a university of her choice, in a subject she would relish, she would have to resit her A levels at a private tutor's academy - and sacrifice the option of spending a Gap Year on overseas travel or voluntary service.(she was not alone among Godalming College students who faced this outcome!).

She buckled down to this course over the autumn and winter of 1984/85, only to suffer a severe attack of gastroenteritis when the time to retake the A Levels approached. She could not do the resits; and was thrown back on a search for a university place on the strength of her Godalming College results. She eventually settled on a place at the University of the West of England (formerly Bristol Polytechnic) to read media studies, It was not an option she viewed with any enthusiasm; but she decided to give it a go, and hope that the combination of good friends and engaging course work would take her forward to rewarding new possibilities. That hope would not be disappointed.

171

******

By the time Karin reached her thirteenth birthday, Nick had left Godalming College on the start of his long journey through Medical School. One consequence of his departure from home was that Karin became closer to Andrew. They formed an increasingly close bond through their teenage years - and beyond. Karin greatly admired Andrew's bold spirit and independent-minded character. And he was always happy to look to Karin for small but important gestures of support. This "alliance" probably made Karin, in her turn, bolder in confronting Mamma and me on issues where we disapproved of her behaviour (or felt that she spent too much of her time socialising!). In a subtle but significant way this altered the family dynamics. And when Nick returned home on holiday breaks, Karin's relations with him became warmer and more confident than when she was just "little sister".

Once Karin had left home to study at Bristol, all our children had temporarily abandoned Groton and set their feet on their adult careers (though they were careful to ensure that there would be a familiar bedroom to return to when they were back on holidays.) Berit and I did not feel too severe a wrench. We felt optimistic that each of the young was ready to embrace an independent life whilst remaining in close and loving contact with their parents. That was, surely, reward enough for us both.

AWB
August 2021

Berit and Alan on our wedding day in
Bromma Church, Sweden,
March 1959

Berit with Nick

Nick and Andrew

Bakersgate Pool with Nick
and Mimi

Mummy with Karin at
Groton 1966

Nick, Andrew and Karin,
Groton 1966

Nick Andrew Karin and
Cousins James and Sarah,
1966

Nick, Andrew and Karin
with Berit and Alan, 1968

Nick Andrew and Karin at
Groton, 1968

Andrew and Karin 1969

Nick and Andrew

Nick, Andrew, Karin and Alan
in Dalarna, Sweden 1971

Andrew and Nick at Groton
1971

Andrew and Nick in Groton
garden

Nick, Andrew and Karin
with Katja the dalmatian

Nick, Andrew and Karin at
25th wedding celebration
dinner

APPENDIX

In Place of Strife: Recollections of Sir Conrad Heron, former Permanent Secretary to Department of Employment.

FOREWORD

I was lucky enough to be one of those who were closely involved in Barbara Castle's courageous attempt in 1968-69 to curb the irresponsible excesses of shop-floor trade union power. She was an acknowledged member of the left wing of the Labour Party, but was clear-sighted and public-spirited enough to accept that it was up to her to try and deal with the problem, in spite of the obvious political risks and difficulties. This is a great tribute to her; and it made the work entailed that much more interesting and even exciting for the officials involved. I acknowledge that I ought long ago to have attempted my own record of the episode for family and friends, and it's quite fortuitous that I've done so now. I was asked by Anne Perkins, Barbara Castle's biographer, to take part in an interview, parts or all of which were to be incorporated in a programme dealing with "In Place of Strife" for broadcast in May '05. Knowing how knowledgeable she was about the central events and the relevant background, I realised that, before being interviewed, I needed to go over and refresh my own recollections, sort them into some sort of order, and do a good deal of background reading to fill in the gaps. This preparation helped me with the interview, and I then wondered whether the knowledge and opinions I had stocked up, could be put to any further use. That led to a talk, which I gave in the Lydford Parish Room in January '05 to help raise funds for its refurbishment and, at the suggestion of some of my audience, to this printed version, which gives a rather fuller account than I could squeeze into my talk.

My own recollections are the main source of the following pages. I found, as I have before, that one memory triggers off another in the most surprising way. It brings back images and incidents which one realizes have lain dormant for decades. I have also used Anne Perkins' biography of Barbara Castle, largely to fill in gaps in my knowledge of Barbara's life before she came to the Department of Employment, and as a counterpoise to gossip, some of it rather ungenerous, from Victor Feather. In Barbara's own diaries, I found a rich quarry of information on what went on inside Cabinet - an aspect of the episode on which she was singularly discreet in her dealings with departmental officials. I have also found Peter Jenkins's account, "The Battle of Downing Street" a very useful guide. I have used Cabinet Office records, particularly those of the talks with the TUC.

CFH, April 2005 (revised March 2008).

In April 1968 I was one of two Deputy Secretaries in the Department of Employment (DEP for short, but previously, and more familiarly known as the Ministry of Labour). I was in charge of the Department's Industrial Relations Department and a few other bits and pieces, but IR, as it was known for short, was my main responsibility. I had got there largely by accident - the accident of being in a particular seat at a particular time. It had fallen to me to conciliate in a number of industrial disputes. My success rate was no better than can be expected: "you win some, you lose some", but, in a field of operations which had more than the normal quota of inflated and prickly egos, I had apparently not caused any major upsets; and had acquired a reputation, which was undeserved, for being patient and even tempered. The truth was that I could just make my limited store of patience last out while I was at work, and my unfortunate wife and children had to cope with a husband and father whose patience was exhausted by the time he got home.

In April 1968 Barbara Castle became our Minister. The previous incumbent, Ray Gunter, had been plain Minister for Employment. Her appointment was as "First Secretary of State and Secretary of State for Employment and Productivity". That marked her out as one of the acknowledged heavyweights in Cabinet: in fact fourth in the pecking order after the Prime Minister, the Chancellor and the Foreign Secretary. Pondering on her unusual title, and the reputation she had won in her previous ministerial jobs, I and others in DEP guessed that we were in for a period of high profile and probably tempestuous activity.

In 1968, we had a Labour Government under Harold Wilson. Labour had come to power in 1964 ·with a wafer-thin majority of five, but a cleverly timed snap election in 1966 had increased Labour's majority to ninety-seven. The country's economic performance was dismal. Year after year, pay increases outstripped the growth of productivity. We had a very large adverse balance of payments. Repeatedly we had had to go, cap in hand, to the International Monetary Fund, for loans to bale us out; and the IMF was getting impatient with the patient's failure to show any signs of economic recovery. The pound was shaky. In 1967 we had had to devalue by almost 15%.

Indisputably, one of our central problems was the chaotic state of industrial relations. The number of strikes had almost trebled over the past decade, and topped 1500 in the year. A few were big official affairs like the seamen's strike in 1966, which precipitated the devaluation of 1967. Most strikes, however, were unofficial, i.e. not authorised by the union(s) concerned, and unconstitutional, i.e. in breach of the procedure agreement negotiated by the employer and the union(s) concerned. Usually, these stoppages occurred with little or no notice, and no prior attempt to negotiate a settlement. A shop steward would call out on strike a small group of workers, but because mass production systems depended on an uninterrupted supply of components, a whole plant could be abruptly halted, and hundreds, or even thousands , of workers in the strike-bound plant and in component-supplying plants could be thrown out of work. Not only the strikers but also those laid off because of the strike would be ineligible for unemployment benefit. The official union attitude, particularly that of the more militant unions, towards these strikes was often one of benevolent ambivalence or even barely concealed connivance. Employers often decided to cut their losses and settle, and concessions from employers were what the unions were in business for. There was no cost to the union; the strikes being unofficial, the unions did not have to pay strike benefit. There was widespread concern, even among trade union members, about the damaging impact of such strikes on the other workers affected and on the economy. There was also considerable public pressure for some restraints to be placed on these irresponsible exercises of trade union power.

The Conservative opposition had issued a comprehensive policy paper, entitled "Fair Deal at Work", setting out their proposals for bringing trade union activity within the law. There had been no commitment from the Government to try and reform industrial relations and it was uninviting ground for a Labour Government to venture on. In one sense, the trade union movement was the senior partner in what was loosely called "the labour movement". The contributions of union members were the main source of Labour Party funds and the block voting system made them the dominant influence at the annual Labour Party conference both in policy discussions and in elections to the Party's national executive committee (NEC). It was inevitable that a Labour Government needed to tread very warily in anything affecting the trade unions.

Nevertheless, Barbara Castle's predecessor, Ray Gunter, had started the ball rolling. Although an ex-trade unionist, he was convinced of the need for reform; and with the agreement of Cabinet had appointed in 1965 a Royal Commission under the chairmanship of a distinguished judge, Lord Donovan. Its terms of reference asked it "to enquire into the state of relations between managements and employees, and into the role of trade unions and employers' organisations in promoting the interests of their members and in contributing to the economic advance of the nation". This last phrase was a clear invitation to the Commission to look into the impact of stoppages on the economy, and into the problem of keeping pay increases in step with productivity. They were also asked to look into the law as it affected trade unions and employers' organisations. The Commission laboured for three and a half years. Its report, published in June 1968, was a decidedly damp squib, and did nothing to meet the widespread demand for urgent action. It reached the obvious conclusion that ,in major sectors of industry, relations at plant level were in a chaotic state, and that a root and branch review of negotiating and disputes procedures was urgently needed. But it concluded that this could only be done by managements and unions, and would take time. The Commission saw no role for Government or any other outside agency in this process, such as suggesting model agreements, and monitoring progress. They saw no case for giving the law a greater role in industrial relations. Their only recommendation - and then a singularly half hearted one - for immediate Government action was the setting up of a standing Commission on Industrial Relations (CIR). But the Commission was to enquire only into matters referred to it by the Government, and would have no independent power to initiate inquiries; also there should be no provision for statutory enforcement of any of its recommendations.

If the Commission had offered even a hint of the need for a more interventionist approach there would have been a useful springboard for government action; but as Ian MacLeod, spokesman for the Conservative opposition and a previous Minister of Labour put it, the report was a "blueprint for inaction." It put the government in a difficult tactical position. Had the commission recommended a substantial raft of measures, the government would have been able to argue that anything less was letting the unions off lightly. But Donovan's "blueprint for inaction" would enable the unions to argue with some plausibility that any serious Government proposals for reform were flying in the face of the expert advice that the Government itself had commissioned.

What of the lady whom Harold Wilson had chosen to fill the ministerial post which her predecessor had described as "the bed of nails"? Barbara Castle had been MP for Blackburn since 1945. She had held two previous ministerial appointments, Overseas Development and Transport. She had made a name for herself as an energetic minister, with ideas of her own, which she was willing, indeed anxious, to test in vigorous debate with officials or anyone else; but once her mind was made up, she was known to be difficult to shift. She was effective particularly with the opposition - she knew it earned her "Brownie points" with her back benchers-- but she could also be abrasive with troublemakers on her own side. She had left her mark on both the Departments in which she had served. When she took over Overseas Development, trading opportunities for UK firms were an important consideration in the allocation of aid to third world countries. She insisted that the primary consideration should always be the needs of the country concerned. At Transport, she introduced the breathalyser - although she never drove a car. She also pursued the romantic dream of a centrally planned, integrated transport system, but got no farther than defining the theoretic goal, namely that the most economic means of transport should be used. Fortunately her move to DEP saved her from drowning in the hopeless morass of defining the criteria for deciding which means of transport was the most economic and the impossibility of reconciling centralised decision making with customer preference.

Barbara was 58 when she came to the DEP. She was small, slight and good looking. She had a wicked smile and a mass of red-gold hair - the original colour was now maintained by twice-weekly visits to a fashionable Knightsbridge hairdresser, which had to be squeezed in whatever the pressure of work. Indeed, her devoted private secretary, Douglas Smith, regularly took letters for signature and other work to these hairdressing sessions. She was always smartly groomed and well, though showily, dressed. She preferred bright reds, yellows and greens. You were not likely to overlook her in a crowd. She was a born interventionist: face her with any problem, her instinctive reaction was "What should I be doing about it?" In some ways, she was a hopeless romantic, for example in her dream of an integrated transport system. She was also a hard-boiled realist. There will be plenty of evidence of that in the following chapters.

She had been a prominent member of the "keep left" group within the Labour Party, led by Aneurin Bevan. For them, Attlee and Gaitskell after him were too slow in implementing a socialist agenda. They also held that the confrontational stance adopted by the USA and the UK towards Russia simply increased Russian intransigence, made higher expenditure on defence inevitable, curtailed resources available for development of the social services, and even caused back tracking on some of the advances already made:for example, the introduction by the Attlee government of charges for spectacles and dentures: the first breach in the cherished principle of a wholly free National Health Service, which led to the resignations of Aneurin Bevan and Harold Wilson.

Barbara had been born in 1910 into a family where the very air she breathed was impregnated with socialism. Her father, Frank Betts, was a tax inspector, but for him his civil service job was simply the guarantee of the modest financial security which enabled him to pursue his real interests: first and foremost, politics, but also amateur dramatics and languages (he taught himself classical Greek, and he dabbled in old Norse). He was an active member of the Independent Labour Party, then still affiliated to the Labour Party, and edited their local paper, the "Pioneer". He believed in the inevitable and imminent decay of the capitalist system and its replacement by a planned socialist economy; and he thrust these beliefs on his three children of whom Barbara was the youngest. He also pushed his children hard academically. At school Barbara had been a slow starter, but she blossomed in her final years at Bradford Grammar School and got three distinctions in her Higher School Certificate, the forerunner of to-day's A levels. She went on to St Hugh's at Oxford, where she read PPE (politics, philosophy and economics). Living away from home for the first time, she flung herself into a hectic social life - she must have been a very attractive young woman - pursued by a long trail of admirers. To her bitter disappointment, she only got a third class honours degree. But she made her mark in the university Labour Club. She spoke often, and took a leading part in the demonstrations which the club organised to protest against Ramsay Macdonald' s defection from the Labour Party in the 1931 financial crisis to join the Conservatives and a few Liberals in the "national government", which introduced a harsh policy of retrenchment, including a 10% cut in the dole on which three million unemployed then depended.

With mass unemployment, and only a third class degree to her name, Barbara was not the brightest of employment prospects; and to keep the wolf from the door she had to settle for a job as a sales representative for a Manchester firm of dried fruit importers(where, incidentally, trade union membership meant the sack). But Barbara was already set on a political career and alongside her job she was working hard at her political apprenticeship. She got plenty of practice in public speaking at the local Labour party meetings. At one of these, the visiting speaker was William Mellor: then editor of the Daily Herald, the national daily identified with the Labour Party, and later the prime mover in the Socialist League, a leftist group fighting for a more radical Labour Party. Shortly after they met, almost as a gesture of defiance to convention, they embarked on a semi-public affair, which was to last until his death 10 years later. As an affair, it was unsatisfactory. He was nearly twice her age, had married some twelve years previously, and had only recently become a father. He kept assuring Barbara that he would get a divorce and they would marry, but it never happened. The affair was however an essential part of her political education , since through it she got acquainted with the inner workings of the Labour party and with many of its national figures. Two years after his death, Barbara married Ted Castle, who was then a journalist working on Picture Post and the Mirror. He was big, laid back, sociable and had a bit of a drink problem. She was highly-strung, insecure and highly critical of whatever she did. It was a tempestuous marriage, but it proved durable, and on the whole, it was a happy one. He was a good prop and comforter when she was feeling depressed. To her great regret, and, I think, his, they had no children, but Barbara was a wonderful aunt to her sister's brood.

"IN PLACE OF STRIFE" TAKES SHAPE.

Barbara Castle was carrying a staggering load of work at this time. On my side of the house, discussion of negotiating tactics in disputes, briefing her for personal interventions, and questions in Parliament took up a large slice of her time. She had a similar load on incomes policy, responsibility for which had been added to the Department when she came.

In an attempt to keep pay increases in line with productivity, successive governments in the 60s and 70s set norms for pay increases varying from 0 to $3\frac{1}{2}\%$, any extra to be conditional on greater productivity. Settlements affecting 50 workers or more had to be reported; and the Government had power to put a standstill order on settlements which appeared excessive, and to refer them to a Prices and Incomes Board for detailed examination. This could lead to their being given the go-ahead or to continuation of the standstill order. These policies required considerable staffing resources and were never more than partially successful. They generated a heavy burden of case work and parliamentary work, much of which landed on the Secretary of State's desk.

Last and most important in Barbara's workload was the problem of devising measures to try and curb the prevailing industrial anarchy, and a strategy for getting them from the drawing board into operation.

Denis Barnes, my permanent secretary, and I had long been convinced that trade unions, like all powerful subjects, should be brought within the law. We had talked exhaustively of possible measures in the belief that one day it was bound to happen, and we could pull out of our bottom drawers studies of precedents in legislation in other countries for measures like compulsory strike ballots and standstill orders on industrial action. As I have mentioned, despite the appearance of the Conservative Party's policy paper, "Fair Deal at Work ,"proposing a comprehensive legal framework for the improvement of industrial relations, nothing similar had so far figured in the Labour Government's programme; and, frankly; before Barbara Castle, we had not had a Minister with the ability, the political clout, and the courage to take it on. But after the initiation, which she had undergone, Barbara needed no more convincing; and we had the unprecedented and heartening phenomenon of a Minister, closely identified in the past with the left wing of the Labour Party, now persuaded by her first hand experience that industrial relations reform was needed. Though conscious of the formidable obstacles to be overcome and of the risks to her own political career, she was convinced that it was up to her to make a start. Courage of that order is a rare commodity.

So Barbara launched into discussions with officials. At the outset, we, that is the officials concerned, argued two basic premises. The first was that the Donovan recommendations, with the exception of the appointment of the Commission on Industrial Relations, were of no help. The second was that the TUC was incapable of delivering a solution. The TUC, i.e. the General Council and its supporting bureaucracy, was the creature of the affiliated unions, particularly of the big and powerful unions, rather than their master or even their pilot. The unions had ceded to the TUC limited powers for dealing with inter-union disputes, (both the "who-does-what" and the "member-poaching" kind), and in the main, the arrangements had worked well. George Woodcock, then TUC General Secretary, was convinced that "Let's just squeeze as much as we can out of the employers and the government " was not an adequate philosophy for a trade union movement which claimed to be a responsible partner together with employers and government in a democratic society committed to the maintenance of full employment, economic advance and progressive improvement in social provision. Woodcock had asked the annual Congress to address itself to the question: "What are we here for?" but there had been no rush to attempt an answer. He had also won the unions round to grudging acceptance of the need for an incomes policy, but only as a temporary emergency measure; and they were determined to shake it off as soon as possible. The tradition of union autonomy was strong, and there was never any hope that member unions would accept the degree of TUC interference necessary to secure adherence to an industrial relations code of behaviour, which balanced their rights with their responsibilities to the community. Nor was there any hope that the two powerful buccaneers now at the helm of the transport and engineering unions (TGWU and the AEU) would allow the TUC to circumscribe what they saw as their legitimate activities. So, it had to be Government action or nothing.

When the main outlines of the proposals, which were later to be embodied in a White Paper were clear, Denis Barnes suggested to Barbara that, before further work was undertaken, it would be prudent for Barbara to make certain that she had the solid backing of the PM; and, assuming she got a satisfactory answer from him, it would be worthwhile taking George Woodcock into her confidence and getting his assessment of the likely reaction of the unions. We assured her that, on past form, Woodcock could be trusted to keep the information to himself. Barbara came back from her talk with Harold Wilson much encouraged. He thought her proposals would be beneficial for the economy, and, by demonstrating that the Government was prepared to tackle the problems of industrial anarchy, its authority would be enhanced-- and the party's chances of being returned at the next election would be improved. He assured her of his total backing. On then to Woodcock. His assessment of the unions' reaction to the proposals was that they would "huff and puff", but at the end of the day, they would stomach the package. He was doubtful, however, whether any great good would come of Barbara's proposals. His doubts were of a piece with his general approach to the question of reform of industrial relations. He had been a member of the Donovan Commission and was a firm believer in the wholly voluntary approach to the problem, which the Commission had recommended. He accepted that there were a few basic measures which a benevolent government could enact, and which would be beneficial to trade union members, such as minimum wage legislation, a statutory right to belong to a trade union, and a statutory mechanism to enable unions to secure recognition; but he saw no role for the government or the law in the collective bargaining process.

Woodcock wanted desperately to become the first chairman of the Commission on Industrial Relations, a post from which he hoped to engage the unions in debate on his fundamental question, which they had left unanswered: "What are we here for?" At her meeting with Woodcock, Barbara broached the question of the CIR Chairmanship with Woodcock, and told him he was the front runner for the post, which was in her gift (subject to the PM's endorsement). The appointment was duly announced in midJanuary '69. But one consequence of the appointment was that Woodcock's deputy, Victor Feather, became acting and later substantive General Secretary of the TUC - a change which did not bode well for Barbara.

By mid-October '68, Barbara's ideas had taken fairly definite shape, and she was anxious, before taking them further, to test them in wider debate, but on a confidential basis. For this purpose a week-end conference was arranged at the Government conference centre at Sunningdale in November '68. It was attended by a handful of carefully chosen politicians, some civil servants, and a few trusted outsiders - all sworn to secrecy. The proposals, which were subsequently to be enshrined in White Paper, were aired as very tentative ideas, still subject to alteration, amendment, and even to be dropped, but nevertheless a worthwhile basis for discussion. The proposals got a good reception; there were no convincing objections, and no suggestions for substantial change. At the final session, Barbara gave a masterly summing-up, which was, in fact, an outline of the White Paper to come. Sadly, but hardly surprisingly, although all had pledged themselves to secrecy, leaks that the meeting had taken place, and of the substance of some of the proposals appeared in the press. There were some ruffled feathers among Barbara's Cabinet colleagues, claiming to be outraged that she had had discussions about possible legislation affecting the unions of which Cabinet as a whole had no knowledge. Was she trying to face them with a fait accompli?

Barbara faced a further "no win" dilemma: whom should she start formal discussions with first, the Cabinet or the TUC and in parallel, of course, the employers' organisation, the Confederation of British Industry (CBI)? If she went to Cabinet first, it was certain, given the close links between certain of her Cabinet colleagues and the TUC, that the TUC would have the full text of her Cabinet paper very shortly after the paper was circulated and before it was discussed by Cabinet; and predictably, by the following day at the latest, there would be bitter complaints that it was preposterous of Barbara to put to her colleagues full blown proposals for legislation, in which the unions were the party primarily concerned, without having consulted them first. If she went to the TUC first, there would be similar outrage from colleagues that they had not been given first bite. Barbara opted for going to the TUC first on the ground that with Harold's promised support, it was reasonable to expect that Cabinet would endorse the proposals; and as the ultimate argument would be with the TUC, it was wiser not to kick off by giving them an excuse for playing the offended party.

The proposals, now in the form of a draft White Paper had a fairly sticky passage, first through a specially appointed steering committee, the Management Committee, and then through full cabinet. There were some injured egos among those who had not been on the Management Committee, and this led to a plague of nit-picking amendments, suggested by Crossman and others. Nearly all of these Wilson and Barbara successfully batted away, and very few found their way into the final version of the White Paper; but there was a rumble of more serious opposition from Jim Callaghan. He was then Home Secretary, a post to which he had been moved after a rather undistinguished spell as Chancellor (during which the 1967 devaluation had occurred). An ex-trade unionist (he had been general secretary of the Inland Revenue Staff Federation), he had made a point of cultivating very close relations with the unions. He also had his eyes on the seat presently occupied by Harold Wilson. His attack was not about the merits or demerits of the proposals, but simply that they risked damaging the unity of the "labour movement", and avoiding that should be the Government's paramount concern. His experience at the Treasury should have taught him that dancing to the unions' tune was the highway to traumas like the 1967 devaluation of the pound.

Cabinet did eventually approve the draft White paper, but one tiny amendment slipped in, which was to be of vital importance in the discussions which were to follow with the TUC. The White Paper announced that the Government intended to have consultations on the proposals with the TUC and CBI with a view to legislation. The amendment slipped in was the insertion of the words "unless an equally effective and urgent alternative can be found. "It opened a loophole which the TUC were to exploit with disastrous effect. The established convention is that the Cabinet minutes do not record numbers for and against, but towards the end of the final discussion, Harold slipped a note to Barbara on which he had scribbled "16 -7."

The White Paper entitled "In Place of Strife" was published on 15th January '69. The title had been suggested by Ted Castle. It was chosen in the hope that it would have a special resonance for the Labour left wing. One of their icons was a pamphlet "In Place of Fear" from the pen of Aneurin Bevan, which set out in popular style his contention that negotiation with Russia instead of confrontation would make possible cuts in defence expenditure and release resources for better social provision.

After rehearsing the current unsatisfactory state of industrial relations and giving a cursory nod to Donovan, the White Paper proposed a judicious mix of measures: on the one hand sweeteners for the unions (though they were presented as measures to strengthen the unions and help them restore order in their own house), and on the other, measures to give the Government powers to deal with unofficial and unconstitutional strikes. The proposed measures to "strengthen the unions" were a statutory right to belong to a union, and a power to enable the Minister to require an employer to recognise and negotiate with a union, but only to be exercised to give effect to a recommendation made after investigation by the CIR. If the employer then refused to enter into meaningful negotiations, the union would have automatic access to arbitration, and the award given legal force. On the other side, the Minister proposed to seek power, to be used when a stoppage of work might have serious repercussions, to impose a 28 day "conciliation pause", during which there would be a compulsory return to work on "status quo ante" terms (something which unions had been fighting for for over fifty years) and during which a solution to the dispute would be sought by all available methods -negotiation, conciliation, inquiry, arbitration, help from the CIR and TUC, nothing was ruled out. If workers disobeyed the order to return to work, they would suffer a financial penalty. If they refused to pay the penalty, and persisted in refusing in defiance of a specific court order, this could, under the law as it stood, and in the absence of special provision, eventually lead to imprisonment. In order to prevent "refusenik" strikers becoming martyrs, the White Paper proposed that, in the last resort, court orders should be made for the attachment of earnings, i.e. the compulsory deduction of the penalty from earnings. A power to impose a compulsory strike ballot was also proposed. Finally, in inter-union disputes which the TUC had been unable to resolve, there would be a power to refer the problem to the CIR and to give legal force to their recommendation.

Press reaction was generally favourable. The Times leader commented that "the compulsory measures are the least that any government could put forward in the present climate of public opinion... the unions would be foolish indeed if they tried to work up resistance to the proposals ... the compulsory powers need never be used if the unions put their own house in order. " Curiously, in the same edition, Eric Wigham, the Times industrial correspondent, who had been a member of the Donovan Commission and was wedded to their voluntary approach, was less sanguine. He had doubts whether the proposals would reach the statute book, and if they did, whether they would be effective. Opinion polls recorded substantial majorities in favour of the proposals: and could there have been a referendum, they would no doubt have been resoundingly endorsed. During the months following publication of the White Paper, when Barbara was in the thick of the battle to get her proposals off the drawing board and onto the statute book, she nevertheless undertook a punishing speaking programme to expound her proposals. She went whenever there was a gap in her schedule, and wherever she was invited or could engineer an invitation -to the Scottish TUC, to several union annual conferences, to regional trade union meetings, and to a number of factories.   She would make a point, when meeting shop stewards, if possible without management representatives present, that the legislation could enhance the opportunities of union representatives to improve workers'rights and conditions. She spoke with vigour and conviction, and got standing ovation after standing ovation. On many occasions, individual trade union members and officials felt moved to come up to her at the end of a speech to congratulate her on the White Paper, and urge her to stick to her guns and see the proposals through. But the fate of the White Paper was to be decided not by the views of the general public or of ordinary trade union members, but in protracted argument between government and trade union establishment, by opinion in the Parliamentary Labour Party(over 130 of whom were sponsored by trade unions*), and by a divided Cabinet, some members of which gave precedence to their trade union sympathies over their Cabinet loyalty.

The personalities of the main players on the trade union side were to be of major importance in the drama about to unfold.Jack Jones and Hugh Scanlon were the two most powerful figures on the trade union side, and no settlement between government and TUC could be arrived at without their agreement. Although very different characters - Scanlon ebullient and out going, Jones introverted and dour - both had started their trade union careers as shop stewards, both were anxious to keep close links with the shop floor leadership, and to resist any restriction on the use of their industrial clout. But the central role in the negotiations with the government was to be played by Victor Feather, now acting general secretary of the TUC, but subject to confirmation in the post by the annual Congress in September. It was understandable therefore that he would want to show that he was no "push-over" in the coming consultations on the White Paper, and he would obviously not want to alienate Jones and Scanlon, because of the huge influence the block votes of their unions gave them in the TUC annual Congress and in the Labour Party annual conference. There was however another important factor: the relationship between Vic Feather and Barbara. One had only to see them together for a few minutes to realise that they did not get on and that their mutual dislike had its origins far back in the past. Feather had started his working life as a milk roundsman for the Co-op Dairy in Bradford. He was, of course, a trade unionist and a socialist, and had been prominent locally in the 1926 general strike. Barbara's father, Frank Betts, acted as an unofficial talent spotter for Labour Party and trade union organisations in the area. He also organised cultural activities, such as guided visits to art galleries and museums for young socialists In the course of one of these he became acquainted with Victor, and soon realised that his abilities could be put to better use for the benefit of the labour movement in a more responsible job. Soon afterwards, Victor was taken on by the Distributive Workers' Union ; from there, he moved on to a back room job in the TUC, and by 1968 he had risen to deputy to the general secretary, George Woodcock. Feather made no secret of his contempt for Woodcock 's high falutin' ideas about the need for the trade unions to rethink their role in society; and, no doubt, heaved a sigh of relief when Woodcock moved to the CIR. In the Department, we had got to know Feather over the years and had no doubt of his ability, but he was not a person to whom one took easily. He had an unctuous, cringing manner. He was cunning and devious, and had the cheek of the devil. I used to think that, cast as Uriah Heap**, he would have been a sensational hit. He was going to be a formidable leader of the TUC team, and not well disposed to Barbara.

*Uriah Heap, a character in Dickens' novel, David Copperfield, had in rich measure the less attractive traits of character and manner, which I have ascribed to Feather. As is predictable in Dickens, Heap eventually has his "come-uppance."He is convicted of fraud and transported to Botany Bay, a convict settlement in Australia. Feather, on the other hand, retired in the mid 70s, when all still looked set fair for the unions.

BATTLE IS JOINED

There was no hint of the storms ahead in the first consultative meeting with the TUC's Finance and General Purposes Committee late in January, 1969. They welcomed those proposals which were to the trade unions' advantage - the right to belong to a trade union, statutory machinery for securing recognition and the status quo ante. A mildly worded caveat was registered against what came to be known as the penal clauses. Further comment was deferred until after the next meeting of the full General Council.

The parallel meeting with the CBI. was hardly more informative. They told us that the White Paper proposals, though largely unexceptionable, were, given the size and urgency of the problem, too little, too late; "a nutcracker to split a cannon-ball." This remained the CBI's constant and unhelpful refrain throughout the coming months, changing only to shrill criticism of the Government's weakness after the final denouement.

A protracted series of meetings between the Government and the TUC spread out over the next four and a half months. In parallel, there were numerous private talks with Feather and other trade union worthies. Inside the Government, there were numerous meetings of the Management Committee set up to oversee the progress of the negotiations with the TUC; there were regular reports to the full Cabinet to keep colleagues posted, and hopefully to keep them on side. A special TUC Congress was summoned to consider the TUC's counter-proposals. There was a highly significant private meeting over dinner at Chequers between the PM and Barbara on the Government side, and Feather, Jones, Scanlon and John Newton, the current General Council chairman, on the trade union side. Throughout this period, despite the breath-taking pace of events, and the multiple claims on her time, Barbara insisted on filling even the slightest gap in her programme with additional speaking engagements to expound the White Paper. Unbelievably, Barbara also managed to squeeze in a Mediterranean holiday on a borrowed yacht during the Whitsun Parliamentary recess, but in the event it did not turn out to be the undisturbed relaxation she had hoped. From time to time, there were rumbles of dissent, and threats of breaking ranks from sections of the Parliamentary Labour Party, and from within the Cabinet; and they reached a crescendo as events moved to a climax.

The first signal of impending danger came from a meeting of the Parliamentary Labour Party early in February to discuss the White Paper. Meetings like this are arranged from time to time to give the Minister concerned and the interested party members the opportunity of an off-the-record discussion of a topic of current Parliamentary interest, without the inhibiting presence of members of other parties. At the meeting, reactions to the White Paper were generally complimentary, but there were numerous objections to compulsory strike ballots, the conciliation pause, and the attachment of earnings - in fact to everything which was not a free gift to the unions.

Then there was a minor "spat" between Barbara and Feather. It would have been insignificant but for the fact that it did nothing to improve their already sour relations.Feather had published an address to an East European Communist Party journal which was critical of key aspects of the White Paper; and this had attracted comment in the British press. Barbara insisted on tackling Feather about the unhelpful nature of this intervention.

Feather's lame defence was that it was written only for a Soviet paper, so surely no-one would take it seriously. He urged her to pay little attention to the criticisms, though some were in fact the very arguments which he and the TUC representatives were to deploy in the forthcoming discussions. As he took leave, Feather, turning on his best Yorkshire accent, which he thought endearing and emollient, assured her "Nay, luv, it'll be aalright!."

On 3rd March. at the end of a full day's debate on the White Paper, 53 Labour MPs voted against the Government and an estimated 40 abstained. There were some special circumstances which, it could be argued, had inflated these numbers. After the 1966 election, when the Labour majority had jumped to 97, the party's standing orders had been suspended. This meant that members voting against the Government probably got away scot free; and even in extreme cases, the sanction was unlikely to be more severe than temporary exclusion from party meetings. (With the standing orders in force, as they had been between 1964 and 1966, defection meant being summoned before the Party's National Executive Committee, which, unless there were special extenuating circumstances, was bound by the rules to withhold endorsement at the next election - an almost certain guarantee that the member would lose his seat). The Conservatives had also made it clear that ,on this occasion, they would be abstaining rather than voting against the Government. Thus members who wished to demonstrate their dissent could do so in the knowledge that they faced no disciplinary sanctions and that there was no risk of causing a Government defeat. But the numbers dissenting were undoubtedly a serious shock for the Whips and the Government.

Worse was to follow. The Labour Party National Executive Committee (NEC), met on 19th March. Several Ministers, including Barbara,

George Brown, Callaghan and Wedgewood Benn were members. One item of business was an ambiguously worded draft resolution put forward by Joe Gormley of the National Union of Minerworkers. It called on the NEC to declare that it could not support "any legislation based on all the proposals in the White Paper." Was the NEC being asked to condemn any legislation based on any of the proposals in the White Paper, or was it being asked to say that a package of all the proposed measures was too much to stomach at one go? Callaghan, speaking in support of the resolution, suggested deleting the word "any" for the sake of clarity. Gormley accepted the change without demur. The meaning of the amended text, asking the NEC to declare it could not support "legislation based on all of the proposals in the White Paper,"was still not entirely free from ambiguity; but it seems that in the discussion which followed, it was generally assumed that the draft resolution was asking the NEC to declare its total opposition to the White Paper proposals. Although it had long been accepted doctrine within the Labour Party that NEC resolutions did not bind a Labour Government, Callaghan's attitude was baffling. He had opposed the White Paper in Cabinet, but after it had been formally approved by Cabinet, he was duty bound under the normal Cabinet conventions to support, and at the very least, not to oppose it, particularly in a semi-public forum. Despite frantic pleas from Barbara, (who tried without success to substitute an alternative draft welcoming her plans to hold further consultations with the TUC on her proposals) and from George Brown and Wedgewood Benn (not often on the side of good order and plain common sense) ,the NEC discussion and the resolution became known to thePress, and headlines about the rift within the Cabinet would be blazoned across the following day's front pages. Barbara, aware that Harold Wilson kept a very loose rein on his Cabinet colleagues, and was reluctant to read the riot act at them, telephoned him immediately after the NEC meeting to press him to discipline Callaghan. Harold was on the point of departing for Nigeria on Commonwealth business, but promised that on return a week later he would see Callaghan and "be very tough with him." In the event, what happened when Harold got back was a meeting between him and Callaghan, resulting in a "decision by mutual agreement," as Harold put it, that Callaghan would be dropped from the Management Committee and a very mild homily to Cabinet generally on the undesirability of Ministers giving private briefings to the press. Barbara found this woefully inadequate, but Harold may have been motivated not merely by his distaste for personal unpleasantness, but by the fear that if he pushed Callaghan to the point of resignation, the whole Cabinet might disintegrate.

A further complication was to have an adverse effect on the fortunes of "In Place of Strife." In the spring of 1969, the Chancellor, Roy Jenkins, was having to negotiate a new line of credit with the International Monetary Fund (IMF) in order to meet repayments due on previous loans. As a condition of any new loan, the IMF was demanding a letter of intent from the Government committing it to stringent economic policies, in particular to expenditure cuts and increased taxation, which were bound to increase unemployment and adversely affect the Government's popularity. The Government's dilemma was made more acute by the fact that the statutory powers required for the incomes policy were due to expire at the end of the year, and the near unanimous view of Ministers was that there was no realistic chance of getting sufficient support for their renewal from the Parliamentary Labour Party. This led Roy Jenkins to press for legislation on Barbara's White Paper proposals to be squeezed into the 1969 session of Parliament so he could present them to the IMF as an alternative means of bearing down on wage settlements. This was completely at variance with Barbara's ideas on timetable or the purpose of her proposals. She wanted time to press the case for the White Paper proposals on grass roots trade union and wider public opinion, in the hope that it would make the TUC more receptive. Sadly, Barbara lost the argument in Cabinet and Roy Jenkins announced in his Budget speech in mid April that there was to be legislation on the White Paper proposals, but in a shortened form, which came to be known as the interim bill. Legislation on compulsory strike ballots was to be deferred until a later session, as were proposals on unfair dismissal and financial assistance for training trade union officials, which had been mentioned in the White Paper, not as firm proposals for legislation but as matters for consultation, leading, hopefully, to legislation. at a later stage.

Almost as an appropriate accompaniment to this troubled scene, the rumblings of disputes continued in the background. Two of the more notorious deserve mention, both examples of almost irrational inter-union friction. At the Girling factory in the Manchester area, which made brake sub-assemblies for much of the motor industry, and had an abysmal industrial relations record (57 strikes in the preceding year) a small group of workers belonging to the AEF came out on strike . We slapped on an inquiry, but against the usual pattern of behaviour, the men refused to go back to work while the inquiry was sitting. Two interesting episodes occurred during the inquiry proceedings. First, a deputation of women workers at Girlings, who had been laid off, came to the inquiry to protest about the irresponsible behaviour of their male colleagues. Secondly, it came to our knowledge in the Department that Scanlon himself thought that the strikers, who were members of his union, were behaving unreasonably; and we arranged for him to meet at the Department, four shop stewards who were attending the inquiry-- and that led to a return to work. (In the industrial relations business, you can't afford to be fussy about the quarter you accept help from). The second dispute occurred at the Vauxhall assembly plant at Ellesmere Port. Twelve platers went on strike because a supervisor had had the temerity to open an oil supply valve - an operation. which the platers regarded as their preserve. The strike brought the Ellesmere Port plant to a standstill, and caused some 13,000 workers to be laid off there and in other Vauxhall plants. It almost seemed as if the shop stewards at Girling and Vauxhall were set on underlining the need for something like the "conciliation pause". These two strikes were, of course, both unofficial and unconstitutional, and concurrently, there were plenty other such strikes of lesser importance. Very tellingly, at the next meeting with the TUC, the Prime Minister brandished a copy of the Financial Times of the day, with reports of five wildcat strikes on the front page.

It was against this troubled background that the further talks between the Government and the TUC took place. There were six meetings in all between early April and mid-June. The Prime Minister and Barbara led for the Government; the TUC was represented at the first two meetings by the Finance and General Purposes Committee, but Jones and Scanlon, who were crucial figures on the trade union side, were relative newcomers to the General Council and because of the weight given by the TUC to seniority, were not yet members of the Finance and General Purposes Committee. So the TUC was represented by the full General Council at the last four meetings.

The TUC had moved in a leisurely way on the central recommendation of the Donovan Commission that negotiating and disputes procedures at work place level urgently needed root and branch revision. They had called a few meetings of unions with members in particular industries to discuss the Donovan report, but there had been no signs of energetic follow-up, so that realistically no more than a little progress in a long time could be expected. Unabashed, however, the TUC's basic position set out at the first Government -TUC meeting, and maintained throughout the talks, was that this was a job for managements and unions, and that there was no role for Government: "keep your nose out where you're not wanted" was their blunt message. The Government's response which also remained unchanged throughout the talks was: "We understand and accept that improving negotiating and disputes procedures at works level in our major industries is bound to be a lengthy process, but in the meantime, there is an urgent problem to be dealt with: serious damage is being inflicted on British industry and the nation's economy day by day by wildcat strikes; the White Paper proposals are an attempt to deal with that problem '" And the TUC riposte: the penal clauses are anathema to us; we'll never swallow them. They bring the "taint of criminality into industrial relations" (Feather's exaggeratedly emotive words). To which the Government replied: "We've provided for the payment of fines by attachment of earnings; and if acceptable to the TUC, provision could easily be made for the payments to be made to an approved charity of benefit to workers generally. The TUC's reply: "That doesn't help. Workers would still be penalised, and we're against penalties in any form." So far, remarkably like a dialogue of the deaf.

But the White Paper proposals, though not acceptable to the TUC, did have one important result :they spurred the TUC to produce their own proposals. By the time of the third Govt-TUC meeting in early May, a TUC Special Congress had been called for 5th June to consider the TUC alternative to "In Place of Strife." The TUC document was entitled "Programme for Action." In response, the Government undertook to hold back the interim bill, to allow time for consultation on the outcome of the Special Congress, and to consider whether the TUC had come up with something which could be regarded, in the words which had slipped into the White Paper, as "equally effective and urgent" as its own proposals. Feather had previously given us sight of an advanced draft in confidence, and some of our suggestions for strengthening it were adopted in the definitive version.

The TUC document addressed itself first to the problem of inter-union disputes. The General Council already had power to summon unions involved in an inter union dispute to submit their difference to a Disputes Committee appointed by the General Council, and a union refusing to accept the Committee's ruling could be suspended, and, if necessary, disaffiliated - the ultimate penalty available to the General Council. Additionally, it was now proposed to place unions under an obligation not to authorise a stoppage of work in an inter-union dispute, until the General Council had considered the case; and if a stoppage had already taken place, the union concerned was to be put under an obligation to take immediate and energetic steps to secure a return to work. This went a long way towards meeting the Government's objectives, so far as inter-union disputes were concerned.

The TUC's proposals on unconstitutional strikes., i.e. in breach of an agreed disputes procedure, were less satisfactory. But for the first time, the General Council spelt out that , where there was a proper disputes procedure and the status quo ante was in operation, there should be no stoppage while the dispute was under discussion under the agreed procedure. So far, admirable, but the key question was how was this to be enforced. The TUC's rules already placed an obligation on affiliated unions to keep the TUC informed about disputes, where the effect on other workers was likely to be serious; and a union refusing to accept the General Council's assistance and advice could face suspension and eventually disaffiliation. The rule in question had originally been intended to apply to official disputes, but the TUC now proposed that it should also apply to unauthorised and unconstitutional stoppages. It was also proposed that the General Council would require unions to satisfy them that they had taken all reasonable steps to secure a return to work, "including action under their own rules"- "union speak" for suspending the membership of those who refused to return to work. But not all unions had the necessary powers under their rules to do so. "Some unions may need to revise their rules" continued the TUC document blandly. Not enough said the Government; it ought to be "must, where necessary, revise their rules." That difference was left over for further discussion.

At the next Government - TUC meeting, the Prime Minister and Barbara acknowledged fairly handsomely that the TUC had come a long way to meet them on inter-union disputes, but on unauthorized and unconstitutional disputes, the argument still continued on the "may" or "must" issue. This may seem an absurd semantic difference, but an important and substantial issue lay behind it in the eyes of Jones and Scanlon and others. Whatever the ethical niceties, wildcat strikes had often proved an effective weapon, and any loophole for its use which could be kept open, was not to be lightly thrown away.

A NEAPOLITAN INTERLUDE.

At this point, the story switches from the tedium of the Downing Street discussions, and their accompaniment of stodgy sandwiches and beer; and moves into an episode of pure farce.

Barbara and Ted Castle had a very modest country cottage, Hell Comer Farm, at Ibstone in Buckinghamshire. One of their neighbours, but living in much grander style was Charles Forte, the catering and hotel magnate. Casual encounters developed into friendship. The Castles and Fortes went on walks together, and in the summer of 1968, the Castles had accepted Charles Forte's offer of the use of his yacht, plus crew and domestic staff, for a short holiday in the Mediterranean. They revelled in the luxury. The invitation was renewed in 1969 for a ten day cruise, centring on the bay of Naples, to coincide with the Whitsun parliamentary recess. Barbara, who had been under considerable strain, was very tempted, but hesitant. The risks of adverse publicity were obvious: Barbara living it up as the guest of a hotel and catering magnate on a luxury cruise on his yacht in the Mediterranean, while the TUC are preparing for their Special Congress and the negotiations on the White Paper are moving to a crunch... and so on. But when she mentioned the idea to the PM, he encouraged her to go and take a rest; and to re-assure her that he would do nothing while she was away which might "queer the pitch" on the White Paper negotiations he promised that he would arrange no private meetings with Feather or any-one else, while she was away. If he couldn't decently refuse a request for such a meeting, he would call in the Chancellor, Roy Jenkins, to act as chaperone. (I have some doubts whether this undertaking was observed to the letter). The PM went on to specify that it would be necessary to set up a system of secure communications, preferably encoded, with the yacht so that Barbara could be kept posted of any developments, and if necessary recalled. Feather had aired with the Prime Minister the suggestion of a private dinner party at Chequers with Feather, Jones and Scanlon, and, of course, the PM and Barbara. He claimed it might help to find a way through the difficulties. The PM thought such a meeting might help, but the arrangements had not been finalised or a date fixed. If necessary, Barbara could be brought back from Naples, and taken back after the meeting.

Someone at No 10 must have had fun devising the code names of the main players. The Prime Minister, inevitably, was "Eagle." The temptation to make Barbara "Hawk" must have been very strong, particularly as the press often portrayed her as more hawkish than the PM; but instead she became "Peacock," not the most flattering reference to her penchant for brightly coloured clothes. Feather was "Bear" - which would have been more appropriate for Jones, who became "Horse." "Auntie has got mumps" was the general alarm call, ordering Barbara to return immediately. To make matters even more hilarious, the yacht's radio telephone didn't work, and Douglas Smith, Barbara' s private secretary, was driven to distraction trying to get in touch with her, leaving messages for her to get back in touch with him at various points round the Bay of Naples. Meanwhile, the arrangements for the Chequers dinner party had been firmed up for 1st June. The day before, when still no contact with Barbara had been made, Douglas and I were flown out to Naples by the RAF to find her and bring her back. We did however make a fall-back arrangement before Barbara left that, if she heard nothing to the contrary, she should be at Naples Airport at 1am on 1st June, where there would either be a message waiting for her at the information desk, or some recognisable figure like Douglas or myself. To our immense relief, she was there on time. Then, straight back to Northolt and on to Chequers and the private dinner.

No officials were present at the Chequers meeting, and there is only one full record of the discussion, dictated by the PM the following day. It tallies very closely with Barbara's own account. The atmosphere was friendly, but there was some frank speaking. The meeting had been suggested by Feather, and it soon became clear that his purpose was to show the PM and Barbara the pressure he was under from Jones and Scanlon not to give an inch, so he kept his head down and let them do most of the talking. They had both got their national committees to support the TUC's "Programme for Action," but with difficulty and, in Scanlon's case, with an uncomfortably small majority; and then only on condition that the Government abandoned its own plans for legislation. It became obvious that they were supporting the TUC's plan, not because they backed it as a means of cutting down the number of strikes or improving industrial relations, but in the hope that it would provide a lever to get the Government to abandon the White Paper proposals. At the AEF national committee meeting, Scanlon had been assured by his Midland shop stewards that they could whip up a rash of strikes which would completely swamp the TUC's limited staffing resources and make their proposals for dealing with inter-union and unconstitutional strikes completely unworkable. Jones and Scanlon were totally opposed to any legislation, (except of course those measures which were a bonus to the unions), not merely to the penal clauses; and their real aim in supporting the TUC's proposals was simply to try and stop the Government legislating by the threat that the proposals in "Programme for Action" would be abandoned if the Government went ahead with its interim bill. The PM answered quite firmly that the Government must be free to take what it saw as essential reserve powers, but they could be kept on ice while the TUC put its "Programme for Action" into operation. If the TUC's scheme produced results, there would be no need to activate the measures in the interim bill. They would only be needed to be activated, if the TUC scheme failed. Scanlon and Jones leapt in to suggest that the interim bill should be put on one side for the time being, while the TUC scheme was introduced and allowed to run for a trial period. If it failed, the Government could then revert to legislation. But the PM was too wily to fall into that trap. He pointed out that by the time any judgement could be made about the success or failure of the TUC scheme, the next general election would be imminent; it would then be too late to introduce the interim bill, get it through Parliament, and into operation-- and what a gift it would be to the opposition that the Government was bringing in the legislation, because the TUC scheme had been a flop. It was past midnight when party broke up and went to bed; but not before the PM had a private word with Feather to ask him if he'd got what he wanted out of the discussion. Feather said he had - but that wasn't finding a way through the deadlock.

The following morning, the PM held a short meeting with Barbara, with Douglas and myself in attendance. The PM's view, after the previous evening's discussion, was that "things were about as black as they could be;" but both agreed that it was necessary to keep the threat of legislation hanging over the TUC to get them to tighten up their proposals on unconstitutional strikes. It was agreed that Barbara should send a letter to the TUC spelling out exactly how the Government thought their proposals for dealing with unconstitutional strikes should be strengthened. I was packed off to draft a paper reporting the situation to the Management Committee, and to prepare Barbara's letter, fly out to Naples with it the following day (Tuesday)to get her signature, hurry back and get it to Feather the same evening, so that he should be aware before the TUC's Special Congress on 5th June, that the TUC would need to go a few steps further to satisfy the Government.

So, back hotfoot to the Department to draft the paper for the Management Committee and Barbara's letter to the TIJC. I cleared both drafts with Denis Barnes. We both felt it would be a wise precaution to get the PM to agree both documents, but particularly Barbara's letter to the TUC. That hurdle cleared, I was ready to be flown back to Naples the following morning by the RAF. I was picked up by our Consul from Naples at the airport and whisked off to Herculaneum, where Barbara and Ted were looking round the ruins. Over lunch, she looked over the letter to Feather, which I'd brought for her to sign. She had no quarrel with the substance, but to my intense annoyance she started tinkering with the wording, disregarding completely the crucial fact that the text had been agreed by the PM. Providentially, for dealing with just such an emergency, I had taken some blank sheets of blue embossed Ministerial stationery with me, and I got her signature on a blank sheet positioned to follow the closing paragraph of her amended text. Then back to London, re-submitted the text to the PM, who, thank goodness accepted it without demur, then off it went to Feather by special delivery. The letter set out what the Government regarded as the additional strengthening needed in their proposals for dealing with unconstitutional strikes. There were two main requirements. Firstly, those unions without powers to take disciplinary action against their members should seek the necessary powers, by amendment of their rules if necessary. Secondly, where the General Council had recommended a return to work, and persuasion by the union had failed to secure this, the union should be required to take action under its rules, including the exercise of the union's disciplinary powers against the recalcitrant strikers. If the union failed to do so, the General Council should instruct the union to do so, and failing a satisfactory response, would set in motion its own disciplinary sanctions against the union. A procedure on these lines would, hopefully, make it difficult for unions to go through the motions of instructing their members to return to work, while tipping them off sub rosa to stay out on strike in the hope that the employer would concede the strikers demand: in which case, the TUC was unlikely to go ahead with its own disciplinary procedure against the union.

Barbara's letter was an unpleasant shock for Feather. He had worked hard to get the General Council's agreement to "Programme for Action," but now he was being served notice that if, as expected, "Programme for Action" was endorsed by the Special Congress, it would not be enough to satisfy the Government that the TUC were offering them, in the words of the White Paper, "an equally effective and urgent alternative " to the Government's proposals. Feather decided, nevertheless that getting a clear endorsement of the TUC's Programme for Action was his first priority, and rather than risk muddying the waters at the Special Congress with the Government's further demands, he decided to sit on the letter until after the Special Congress.

The Special Congress ran true to form. The delegates adopted the General Council's document by a 9:1 majority, re-iterated the TIJC's "unalterable opposition" to financial or other penalties, and made a cursory welcoming nod to those of the Government's proposals which were of help to the unions. On the whole the press was impressed by Special Congress and saw in "Programme for

Action" the basis for real forward movement. Their view was deftly captured in a delightful Evening Standard cartoon by Giles. On top of the great lumbering cart horse, which he had long used to symbolise the TUC, were perched the minute figures of the PM and Barbara behind him, with their tiny whips held high, and Harold saying "You know, Barbara, I really think it's beginning to move."

I have often reflected that had mobile telephones and e-mail been available, the business of this episode would have been more easily and expeditiously conducted. Barbara, Douglas and I would have been spared the Northolt-Naples journeys, and settling the text of Barbara's letter to the TUC would have been a lot easier. Unless, of course, the ease of communication which mobile telephone and e-mail have given us, might have encouraged more tinkering, and more paper.

SOLOMON BINDING TO THE RESCUE.

The final stage of the discussions with the TUC was not short of surprises. Favourable press reaction to the TUC's "Programme for Action" and its overwhelming endorsement by the Special Congress had encouraged Labour members to hope that the government would accept the TUC programme, call it a day, abandon the interim bill, and thus avoid exposing a highly public clash between Government and the dissenters in its ranks, which a decision to go ahead with the bill would have provoked. A sharp reminder of the hostility to the White Paper proposals came from the very top of Parliamentary Labour Party early in May. The then chairman of the Parliamentary Labour Party was Douglas Houghton, who had preceded Callaghan as General Secretary of the Inland Revenue Staff Federation, and was Callaghan's close friend and ally. Addressing a meeting of the Parliamentary Labour Party, Houghton urged the Government not to try to push the interim bill through Parliament. "Nothing", he was quoted as saying, "which the bill would do to improve industrial relations, would redeem the harm which we can do to the Labour movement and the nation by the disintegration or defeat of the Labour Party." Worse still, in the meeting of the Management Committee immediately before the resumed discussions with the TUC, it was evident that support for the tough line which the Prime Minister and Barbara proposed to take was ebbing. Crossman warned that, if it came to a break with the TUC, there might well be a split within the Cabinet, possibly a move to install an alternative leadership - presumably Callaghan. Barbara, keeping a watchful eye for waverers, thought that Roy Jenkins, who in a sense had triggered the crisis by insisting on a quick interim bill to placate the IMF, was looking very "shifty." A few however remained solidly on board. Michael Stewart, the Foreign Secretary, slipped Barbara a splendid note; and coming from someone who was rather schoolmasterly and straight-laced, a remarkably forthright one. It read "Anyone who lets you down at this stage is a prize ****"

The negotiating tactics agreed between the PM and Barbara at the meeting the morning after the Chequers dinner party was to hold on to the threat of legislation as a lever to get the TUC to strengthen its proposals for dealing with unconstitutional strikes. At an early stage in the resumed discussions, Brigginshaw, a plausible rogue who ran SOGAT, the biggest printing union, asked the PM if the Government's position was that if the TUC strengthened their proposals on unconstitutional strikes to the Government's satisfaction, the Government would abandon the interim bill. Without a moment's hesitation, or even looking to Barbara for an indication of her view, the PM. said "Yes." This certainly appeared to Denis Barnes and myself, and certainly to Barbara, to be showing the Government's hand earlier and more gratuitously than would have been expected after their discussion about tactics at Chequers. Barbara turned round and muttered to Denis and me, who were sitting immediately behind her "He's given everything away. I'll have to resign!" But she kept a straight face, and in the event didn't - I think because she feared that, if she did, it would rock the boat so violently that it might wreck the Government (and let Callaghan take over) or perhaps lead to a dissolution and an election which the Tories were bound to win.

After the PM's "give-away," it seemed that all that was needed to reach agreement with the TUC was to find a form of words, which would beef up the TUC's commitment to dealing with unconstitutional strikes which would reflect the understanding between the TUC and the Government. But not quite. Because immediately a difficulty arose about the status of any wording which might be agreed. The Government's perfectly understandable position was that any agreed wording should take the form of an addition to, or an amendment of, the rules of Congress. The TUC said blankly that that was not on the cards. That seemed nonsensical. The extension of the General Council's powers envisaged in the TUC document "Programme for Action" was spelt out in the form of substantial additions and amendments to Rule 12 dealing with inter-union disputes, to Rule 11 dealing the unconstitutional strikes and to Rule 13 which dealt with the TUC's disciplinary powers over affiliated unions. Technically, all these changes required confirmation by the annual congress when it met in September, but their endorsement should be a foregone conclusion. It seemed logical that any additional agreed wording to strengthen the TIJC's proposals on unconstitutional strikes should take the same form and have the same status. Although repeatedly pressed the TUC never offered any rational explanation for opposing a rule change. The real reason only emerged much later, in fact, after the negotiations had ended and a deal had been struck with the TUC. It was concerned with the domestic politics of Scanlon's union. He had had difficulty in getting his national committee to agree to support the TUC's "Programme for Action" with the rule changes which the TUC's proposals involved. His assessment was that if he were to go back to his national committee to ask for their agreement to a further rule change, particularly one which might impose restrictions on the use of the shop stewards' favoured weapon, the unconstitutional strikes, he would be turned down. If, however, an agreed form of words could be dished up in some other form than a rule change, he felt he could accept it without going back to his national committee for formal endorsement. He was clearly skating on very thin ice, but he was best placed to judge if it would hold.

So now there were two remaining problems: finding an agreed wording that would commit the TUC firmly enough to action on unconstitutional strikes, and finding a status for it, other than an amendment of or addition to the rules of Congress, but of equal authority. The wording problem was referred to a small drafting committee with members from both sides, and at the third sitting, we reached an agreed text, not plain 'must' instead of 'may,' but the 'the General Council will' and 'the General Council will, if necessary, require the union concerned to...' The Government had given away nothing of substance. It was something of a surprise that the TUC representatives, in the drafting Committee accepted the text, and even more of a surprise that they got the General Council's agreement to it. It may be that Feather, who led for the TUC in the drafting committee, felt that since Jones and Scanlon would do their best, when it came to implementation, to frustrate any effective TUC intervention in unconstitutional strikes, there would be no harm in a tough looking text. It would strengthen the TUC's position vis-a vis the unions and it might help the Government in the very difficult task it would be facing in trying to present the agreement which it now looked like reaching with the TUC as a reasonable return for abandoning the interim bill.

So the score now stood at one down, one still to go. But on that one, there was still no progress. The TUC were adamant that they could not accept amendment of or addition to their rules. They offered to circulate the document to affiliated unions with 'an interpretative statement' from the General Council. But when they were questioned, it appeared that nothing specific would be spelt out about the authority of the document. That was clearly unacceptable to the Government. At that point, the meeting was adjourned until the following morning, to allow the PM and Barbara to report to

Cabinet that evening. It must have been a traumatic session for them. There were murmurs of approval and relief when the PM reported that the TUC had now accepted a strengthened text on unconstitutional strikes. There was even a bouquet from Callaghan to the PM and Barbara. He congratulated them on the considerable progress made thanks to their determination. But then there was a bombshell. Bob Mellish, the Chief Whip, asked leave to speak, (not being a member of the Cabinet), and said he felt he had a duty to warn the PM that he saw no possibility of getting the interim bill through the Commons. From that moment, the interim bill was not only dead but buried. And when the PM and Barbara reported on the remaining impasse over the status of the document, there was dismay and complete incomprehension that they should have baulked over such an inconsequential trifle and blown it up into a sticking point The PM and Barbara quickly found themselves virtually isolated, with an overwhelming majority of the Cabinet (including Jenkins) in favour of accepting the TUC's offer of an "interpretative statement". The PM retorted that if that was the message they wanted taken back to the TUC, they would have to find another messenger. Faced with this threat of resignation, the majority backed off, and the PM and Barbara got authority to negotiate the best deal they could with the TUC the following day, but the Cabinet would remain free to accept or reject any deal they might reach.

Given the speed with which Cabinet news leaked to the TUC, the main figures on the General Council were certainly aware, when discussions resumed the following day ,how shaky the PM's and Barbara's position was in Cabinet. Nevertheless, the PM looked serene, relaxed and confident as he had throughout the discussions. Barbara was steady, but tense. To start with, the TUC continued to stonewall on "no rule change," and in response to repeated probing by the PM offered no rational argument to explain their obduracy. A remark from John Newton, then chairman of the General Council, that they had no wish to commit themselves to something which they couldn't deliver, sounded like a pious and irrelevant platitude, but he might have been hinting at the real obstacle, had we then known how to interpret his remark. Perhaps he was hinting that if the TUC accepted that the agreed wording should become a rule change, then somewhere in the process of collecting the necessary endorsements, there would be a hiccup for example in the AEU National Committee? But we were unaware at that moment of Scanlon's problem, and were unable to guess at the connection. Oddly enough, it was Scanlon who broke the impasse. Out of the blue, he enquired whether an undertaking by the TUC with the same binding force as the Bridlington Principles might offer a solution. The immediate reaction was a puzzled look, on TUC as well as Government faces. Scanlon's suggestion had really been dredged up from the depths of the TUC archives. The Bridlington Principles were a document adopted by the TUC's annual conference, which met at Bridlington in 1939. They were a set of rules designed to stop one union poaching another's members, and for defining in a 'green field' situation, which union or unions might seek to recruit members, and finally a procedure, ending up with the General Council and disciplinary sanctions for dealing with recalcitrant unions. The Bridlington Principles received little notice when adopted - hardly surprising, as their adoption coincided with the outbreak of the Second World War. Poaching disputes reaching the General Council, had been few in number, but they had been successfully resolved. If the Bridlington Principles could not be tampered with, would the TUC give a solemn undertaking, which would have the same binding force as the Bridlington Principles to deal with unconstitutional disputes? The TUC confirmed that it was willing to do so. So we were home and dry --and all that was left to do was to draw up a confirmatory bit of paper covering interunion and unconstitutional disputes, and get formal endorsement of it by the Cabinet(which had been kept on standby and by the General Council, all of which went without any further hitches). "Solemn" and "Binding" were soon merged in Departmental folklore, to become the "Reverend Solomon Binding"- a name which might well have sprung from the pages of one of Trollope's Barchester novels.

The inescapable fact was that it was a humiliating capitulation by the Government. Ministers had been told time and again that the TUC could not deliver, and I believe they accepted our advice; but they were cornered into considering the TUC's counter- proposals met the test set by that little phrase in the White Paper "unless an equally effective and urgent alternative". As opposition to the interim bill built up in the Parliamentary Labour Party, with the help of dissenting Ministers, to a level which made it impossible to get the bill through Parliament, there was no alternative but to try and make the TUC's proposals look as convincing as possible. The words themselves, strengthened by the Government's amendments did indeed look fairly convincing; but it was certain that the big unions would raise constant objections to TUC intervention, and in the end destroy their will and capacity to intervene. In fact, the number of strikes increased substantially during the next year. Barbara herself was put in an impossible position , regularly having to fend off parliamentary questions about disputes in which the TUC should have been carpeting individual unions, but at most were holding exploratory talks with them. I can recall no dispute in which the TUC made use of its extended disciplinary powers. Barbara held weekly meetings with Feather to review current disputes, and find out what the TUC was doing about them; but there were conflicting reports of what was happening on the ground, and disagreements about the need for, and timing of ,TUC intervention. The exchanges between Barbara and Feather often grew acrimonious, and after a few months the meetings were quietly allowed to lapse.

Alan Brown was born at Woking in Surrey in 1934; but spent most of his early years in the Gold Coast (now Ghana), and as a pupil at St Georges School in Cape Town. On his return to England at the end of the Second World War he became a pupil at Bedford School from 1946 to 1952. He saw two years service as a Midshipman in the Royal Navy before going up to Pembroke College, Cambridge to read for a degree in history.

He then enrolled for the degree of Master of Science at the New York School of Industrial and Labor Relations, at Cornell University before entering the British Civil Service as an Assistant Principal in the Ministry of Labour in 1959. It was in this Department that he spent much of his career, with periods on secondment as a senior official to the Manpower Services Commission, the Department of Energy and Health and Safety Executive.

In 1991 he became a Companion of the Order of the Bath. He retired as Director of Health Policy on the Board of the HSE in 1994.